Linda Kephart

Parts of this book appear in *Fodor's Hawaii '92*.

Fodor's Travel Publications, Inc.
New York and London

ISBN 0-679-02061-6

Grateful acknowledgment is made to Richard J. Pietschmann for permission to reprint "Heavenly Hana" and "Highway to Hana" from *Travel & Leisure*, April 1989. Copyright © 1989 by Richard J. Pietschmann.

Fodor's Maui

Editor: Amanda B. Jacobs
Art Director: Fabrizio La Rocca
Editorial Contributors: Suzanne Brown, David Low
Cartographer: David Lindroth
Illustrator: Karl Tanner
Cover Photograph: Dominis/Wheeler Pictures

Design: Vignelli Associates

About the Author

Linda Kephart, a resident of Honolulu, has written articles for *Hawaii Business, Aloha, RSVP, Modern Bride,* and *Pleasant Hawaii.* She is a former editor of *Discover Hawaii.*

Special Sales

MANUFACTURED IN THE UNITED STATES OF AMERICA
10 9 8 7 6 5 4 3 2

Contents

Foreword

We wish to express our gratitude to the Hawaii Visitors Bureau on Maui for its assistance in the preparation of this guide.

While every care has been taken to ensure the accuracy of the information in this guide, the passage of time will always bring change, and consequently, the publisher cannot accept responsibility for errors that may occur.

All prices and opening times quoted here are based on information supplied to us at press time. Hours and admission fees may change, however, and the prudent traveler will avoid inconvenience by calling ahead.

Fodor's wants to hear about your travel experiences, both pleasant and unpleasant. When a hotel or restaurant fails to live up to its billing, let us know and we will investigate the complaint and revise our entries where the facts warrant it.

Send your letters to the editors of Fodor's Travel Publications, 201 E. 50th Street, New York, NY 10022.

Highlights'92 and Fodor's Choice

Highlights '92

A vacation on Maui is more expensive than on any other Hawaiian Island. Over the years, the Valley Isle has established a reputation as a must-see destination for mainlanders; it has been able to capitalize on this reputation by charging high hotel rates. According to a survey done by the national accounting firm Peat, Marwick, Main & Co. in 1988, there were fewer rooms on Maui costing less than $100 a night than on any of its Aloha State competitors.

In late 1990, however, things began to change. Perhaps because of the high prices, Maui's hotel occupancies began to suffer, and the average daily room rate began to come down. Hoteliers responded to declining business by holding steady on the rates. Not under the same pressure, Hawaii's other Neighbor Islands—particularly the Big Island—continued to raise room rates, and the gap began to close.

Hotel News In 1991, construction was completed on Maui's second Hyatt property, a $600 million, 787-room hotel called the **Grand Hyatt Wailea.** Also in Wailea, the **Grand Champions Beach Resort** is slated to offer an additional 426 rooms sometime in 1991, while progress continues on another Embassy Suites, set to open in 1991. The state's second all-suite hotel (the first Embassy Suites opened on West Maui in 1988) will evoke the Mediterranean with white cupolas, archways, and waterways. Ground has finally been broken on the Ritz-Carlton Kapalua construction project, which was delayed when a significant Hawaiian burial ground was discovered under the original site.

Airport Renovations The **Kahului Airport** has been the focus of $41 million in improvements. Work started several years ago, with projects done in phases. A new terminal building was completed by the end of 1990. Phase II was scheduled to begin in 1991 with the conversion of the old terminal into a baggage claim area.

Traffic Patterns If you wonder whether or not to rent a car, consider that Maui has more rental cars per mile of road than anywhere else in the nation. Because of the high visitor counts in the last several years, major rental-car companies have opened their doors on Maui to cash in on the increased business. Moreover, Maui has seen a rapid rise in exotic car-rental companies.

More cars mean more traffic. A few years ago, West Maui tourists found car congestion especially bad during the hours when hotel/resort employees were going to work in the morning and coming home at night. Finally, the county approved a $2 million improvement to the Honoapiilani

Highway, which circles the West Maui mountains from Wailuku to Kapalua. Although traffic can still get congested between Olowalu and Kaanapali, the highway's new third lane eases the situation considerably. A fourth lane is expected sometime soon.

For Art's Sake The long-awaited **Maui Community Arts and Cultural Center** (MCACC) finally broke ground in early 1989, providing a venue for local acting groups as well as major touring companies. The plan for this center began more than 20 years ago and was finally put into motion by corporate backers and a grant from the state. Now MCACC is scheduled to open in early 1992 in Kahului with two theaters—one that will seat 1,150 and an experimental theater with 200 retractable seats. There will also be a 3,500-square-foot gallery space and a gift shop. Both the Maui Community Theatre and Maui Youth Theatre are expected to move into their own satellite wings.

Maui's newest art gallery recently opened in the Valley Island's most unlikely place. Tucked into the luxurious Hotel Hana-Maui, the upscale **Hana Coast Gallery** (tel. 808/248–8636; open daily 9–5) is a joint enterprise between renowned gallery owner Gary Koeppel and beloved Hana author and resident Carl Lindquist. Set in an 1,100-square-foot space, the Hana Coast Gallery exclusively features the work of Hawaiian artists, with some 30% from Hana alone. Tom Faught's enormous ceramic pots, Ron Kent's thinly turned koa bowls, and Betty Hay Freeland's paintings are only a few examples of the creations you'll find here.

Lahaina art galleries have also joined forces in a public effort to create an "art scene" by declaring every Friday night, beginning at 6 PM, as **"Art Night."** Shops stay open late, often offering refreshments to passersby, while strolling musicians add to the cultural ambience. The activity centers on Front Street, but with the burgeoning numbers of galleries the weekly event is spreading to other areas as well.

Fodor's Choice

No two people agree on what makes a perfect vacation, but it's fun and helpful to know what others think. We hope you'll have a chance to experience some of Fodor's Choices yourself while visiting Maui. For more information about each entry, refer to the appropriate chapters in this guidebook.

Beaches

Hana Beach for that Old Hawaii experience

Hookipa Beach to watch world-class windsurfing

Kapalua Beach for sheer class

Little Makena Beach

Wailea Beach in the morning as the sun comes over Haleakala

Best Buys

Fine art, trendy accessories, and T-shirts in Lahaina

Hawaiian quilts

Made on Maui crafts and food

Tedeschi wine right from the vineyards in Kula

Drives

Coming down Haleakala

From Lahaina to Maalaea during whale season

The road to Hana

For Kids

Haleakala Crater

Whale Watching

Lahaina Sugarcane Train

Maui Tropical Plantation

Golf Courses

Kaanapali Resort

Kapalua Golf Club's Bay Course

Wailea Golf Club's Blue and Orange courses

Hotels

Four Seasons Resort *(Very Expensive)*

Hotel Hana-Maui *(Very Expensive)*

Kapalua Bay Hotel *(Very Expensive)*

Maui Inter-Continental Wailea *(Very Expensive)*

Coconut Inn *(Moderate)*

Hana Kai-Maui *(Moderate)*

Kula Lodge *(Moderate)*

Lahaina Hotel *(Moderate)*

Plantation Inn *(Moderate)*

Heavenly Hana Inn *(Inexpensive)*

Kamaaina (Islanders') Favorites

The Makawao Rodeo

People-watching at Longhi's and the Hard Rock Cafe

People-watching at Avalon

Sunrise from Haleakala

Wine tasting at Tedeschi Winery

Local Dining

Fresh fish at Mama's

Maui onion rings at the Maui Onion

Lahaina's trendy "nouvelle Hawaiian" cuisine at Avalon

Shave ice from any roadside stand

Nightlife

Blackie's Bar

Inu Inu Lounge at the Maui Inter-Continental

Old Lahaina Luau

Banana Moon at the Marriott

Restaurants

Raffles *(Very Expensive)*

Plantation Veranda *(Expensive)*

Gerard's *(Expensive)*

Haliimaile General Store *(Moderate–Expensive)*

Lahaina Coolers *(Inexpensive)*

Romantic Hideaways

Candlelight dinner at La Bretagne

Kula Lodge chalets with fireplaces

Royal Lahaina cottage with private pool

Waianapanapa cabins

Sights

Haleakala

Hookipa

Iao Needle

Lahaina Historic District

Wailuku Historic District

Sunsets

From Kimo's in Lahaina

From Kapalua's Bay Club

From the beach at Kaanapali

From the beach at Wailea

Views

All of Maui from Haleakala

Islands of Molokai, Lanai, Kahoolawe, and Molokini

Underwater at Wailea

Waterfalls along the Hana Highway

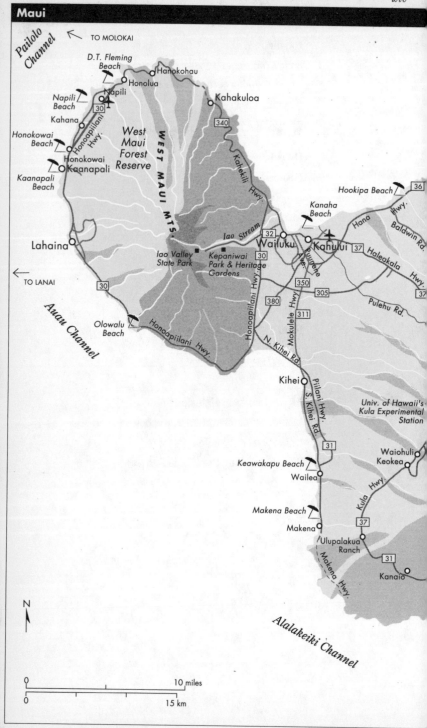

Maui

Pailolo Channel

TO MOLOKAI

D.T. Fleming Beach

Hanokohau

Honolua

Napili

Napili Beach

Kahana

Kahakuloa

Honokowai Beach

30

Honokowai

Kaanapali

Kaanapali Beach

West Maui Forest Reserve

WEST MAUI MTS.

340

Kahekili Hwy.

Hookipa Beach

36

Kanaha Beach

Hana Hwy.

Baldwin Rd.

Lahaina

Iao Stream

32

Wailuku

Kahului

37

Haleakala Hwy.

37

TO LANAI

30

Iao Valley State Park

Kepaniwai Park & Heritage Gardens

30

350

305

Pulehu Rd.

Auau Channel

380

311

Honoapiilani Hwy.

Mokulele Hwy.

Olowalu Beach

Honoapiilani Hwy.

N. Kihei Rd.

Univ. of Hawaii's Kula Experimental Station

Kihei

S. Kihei Rd.

Piilani Hwy.

Waiohuli Keokea

31

Keawakapu Beach

Wailea

Kula Hwy.

Makena Beach

Makena

37

Ulupalakua Ranch

31

Kanaio

Makena Hwy.

N

Alalakeiki Channel

0 _____ 10 miles

0 _____ 15 km

PACIFIC OCEAN

Ulumalu
365
Huelo
Kailua
360
Kaumahina State
Wayside Park
390
Kokomo
Honomanu
Valley
Keanae Arboretum
Makawao
Keanae Overlook
Wailua
Wailua Lookout
Pukalani
Nahiku
377
Waikane
Falls
Haleakala
Crater Rd.
Koolau
Forest
Reserve
360
Hana Hwy.
Waianapanapa
State Park
37
Park
Headquarters
Visitor Center
378
Helani Gardens
Hana Forest Reserve
Hana
Kula Botanical
Gardens
Haleamauu
Trail
Haleakala
National Park
Kaihalulu
Beach
Mt. Haleakala
Haleakala Visitor
Center
Hamoa
Puu Ulaula
Overlook
Kahikinui
Forest
Reserve
Kaupo
Trail
Muolea
Kipahulu
31
Piilani Hwy.
Kaupo
31
Alenuihaha Channel

TO HAWAII

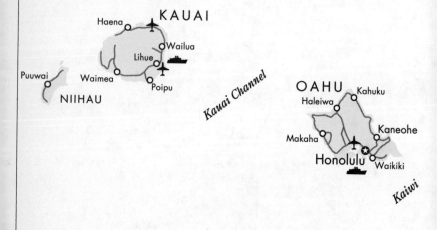

KAUAI

Haena

Wailua

Lihue

Waimea

Poipu

Puuwai

NIIHAU

Kauai Channel

OAHU   Kahuku

Haleiwa

Kaneohe

Makaha

Honolulu

Waikiki

Kaiwi

PACIFIC OCEAN

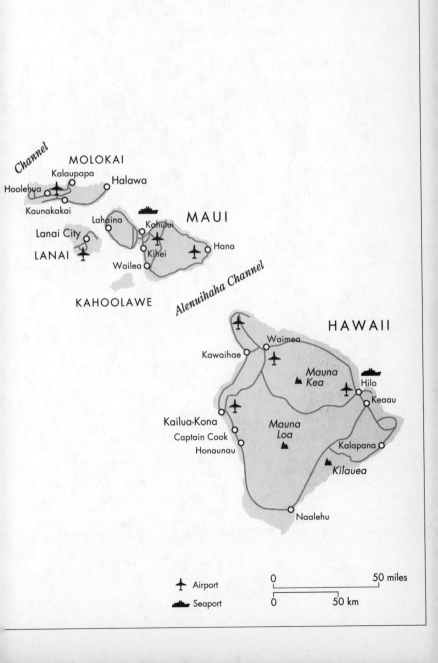

N

Channel

MOLOKAI

Kalaupapa

Halawa

Hoolehua

Kaunakakai

Lahaina

Kahului

MAUI

Lanai City

Kihei

Hana

LANAI

Wailea

KAHOOLAWE

Alenuihaha Channel

HAWAII

Waimea

Kawaihae

Mauna Kea

Hilo

Keaau

Kailua-Kona

Mauna Loa

Captain Cook

Kalapana

Honaunau

Kilauea

Naalehu

✈ Airport

⛴ Seaport

0   50 miles

0   50 km

World Time Zones

Numbers below vertical bands relate each zone to Greenwich Mean Time (0 hrs.).
Local times frequently differ from these general indications,
as indicated by light-face numbers on map.

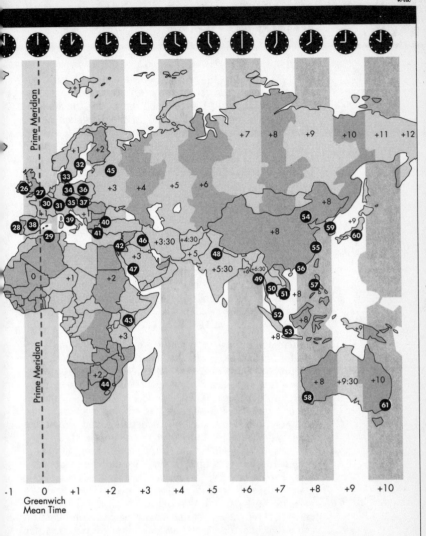

Prime Meridian

+7 +8 +9 +10 +11 +12

+1 +2

+3 +4 +5 +6

+8

+9

+8

Prime Meridian

+3:30 +4:30

+5

+5:30

+6:30

+8

+8

+8

+9

+8 +9:30 +10

0 +1 +2 +3

-1 0 +1 +2 +3 +4 +5 +6 +7 +8 +9 +10

Greenwich
Mean Time

Mecca, **47**	Ottawa, **14**	San Francisco, **5**	Toronto, **13**
Mexico City, **12**	Paris, **30**	Santiago, **21**	Vancouver, **4**
Miami, **18**	Perth, **58**	Seoul, **59**	Vienna, **35**
Montreal, **15**	Reykjavík, **25**	Shanghai, **55**	Warsaw, **36**
Moscow, **45**	Rio de Janeiro, **23**	Singapore, **52**	Washington, D C, **17**
Nairobi, **43**	Rome, **39**	Stockholm, **32**	Yangon, **49**
New Orleans, **11**	Saigon, **51**	Sydney, **61**	Zürich, **31**
New York City, **16**		Tokyo, **60**	

Introduction

Maui, say the locals, is *no ka oi*—the best, the most, the top of the heap. To those who know Maui well, there's good reason for the superlatives. The second-largest island in the Hawaiian chain, Maui has made an international name for itself with its tropical allure, heady nightlife, and miles of perfect-tan beaches. Maui magic weaves a spell over the 2 million people who visit its shores each year and leaves them wanting more. Often visitors decide to return for good.

In many ways, Maui comes by its admirable reputation honestly. The island's 729 square miles contain Haleakala, a 10,023-foot dormant volcano whose misty summit beckons the adventurous; several villages where Hawaiian is still spoken; more millionaires per capita than nearly anywhere else in the world; three major resort destinations that have set new standards for luxury; Lahaina, an old whaling port that still serves as the island's commercial crossroads; and more than 80,000 residents who work, play, and live on what they fondly call the Valley Isle.

Maui residents have quite a bit to do with their island's successful tourism story. In the mid-1970s, savvy marketers on Maui saw a way to increase their sleepy island's economy by positioning it as an island apart. Maui was tired of settling for its meager 50,000 or so visitors each year and decided it didn't want to be one of the gang anymore. So community leaders started advertising and promoting their Valley Isle separately from the rest of the state. They nicknamed West Maui "the Golf Coast," luring in heavyweight tournaments that, in turn, would bring more visitors. They went after the upscale visitor, renovating their finest hotels to accommodate a clientele that would pay more for the best. And they became the state's condominium expert, so that condos no longer meant second-best accommodations. Maui's visitor count swelled, putting it far ahead of that of the other Neighbor Islands.

That quick growth has led to its share of problems. During the busy seasons—from Christmas to Easter and then again during the summer—West Maui can be overly crowded. Although the County of Maui has seen success in its attempts to widen the two-lane road that connects Lahaina and Kaanapali, the stop-and-go traffic during rush hour reminds some visitors of what they face at home. It's not that residents aren't trying to do something about it— the Kapalua-West Maui Airport, with its free shuttle to and from Kaanapali, has alleviated some of the heavy island-circling traffic.

The explosion of visitors seeking out the Valley Isle has also created a large number of businesses looking to make a fast buck from the high-spending segment. Most of the time, the effect is harmless: Lahaina could easily be called the T-shirt capital of the Pacific (in close competition with Waikiki), and the island has nearly as many art galleries and cruise-boat companies as T-shirts. As in other popular travel destinations, the opportunity to make money from tourists in Maui has produced its fair share of schlock.

But then consider Maui's natural resources. The island is made up of two volcanoes, one now extinct and the other dormant, that both erupted many years ago and joined into one island. The resulting depression between the two is what gives Maui its nickname, the Valley Isle. West Maui's 5,788-foot Puu Kukui was the first volcano to form, a distinction that gives the area's mountainous topography a more weathered look. Rainbows seem to grow wild over this terrain as gentle mists move quietly from one end of the long mountain chain to the other. Sugarcane gives the rocky region its life, with its green stalks moving in the trade winds born near the summit.

The Valley Isle's second volcano is the 10,023-foot Haleakala, a mountain so enormous that its lava filled in the gap between the two volcanoes. You can't miss Haleakala (House of the Sun), a spectacle that rises to the east, often hiding in the clouds that cover its peak. To the Hawaiians, Haleakala is holy, and it's easy to see why. It's a mammoth mountain, and if you hike its slopes or peer into one of its craters, you'll witness an impressive variety of nature. Desertlike terrain butted up against tropical forests. Dew-dripping ferns a few steps from the surface of the moon. Spiked, alien plants poking their heads out of the soil right near the most elegant and fragrant flowers.

In fact, the island's volcanic history gives Maui much of its beauty. Rich red soil lines the roads around the island—*becoming* the roads in some parts. That same earth has provided fertile sowing grounds for the sugarcane that has for years covered the island's hills. As the deep blue of ocean and sky mingle with the red and green of Maui's land, it looks as if an artist had been busy painting the scenery with his favorite colors. Indeed, visual artists love Maui. Maybe it's the natural inspiration; maybe it's the slower pace, so conducive to creativity.

Farmers also appreciate the Valley Isle. On the slopes of Haleakala, the volcanic miracle has wrought agricultural wonders, luring those with a penchant for peat moss to plant and watch the lush results. Sweetly scented flowers bloom large and healthy, destined later to adorn a happy brow or become a lovely lei. Grapes cultivated on Haleakala's slopes ripen evenly and deliciously, then are squeezed for wine and champagne. Horses graze languidly on rolling meadows of the best Upcountry grasses, while jacaranda trees dot the hillsides with spurts of luscious lavender. As the big brute of a volcano slides east and becomes the town of Hana, the rains that lavishly fall there turn the soil into a jungle. Ferns take over the forest, waterfalls cascade down the crags, and moss becomes the island's carpeting.

Geologists claim that Maui was created between 1 and 2 million years ago by the eruption of two volcanoes, Puu Kukui and Haleakala; a low central isthmus formed between them and joined them into West and East Maui. The island had no indigenous plants or animals. Birds brought some of the life that would inhabit Maui, as did the tides that washed upon its newly formed shores. Then Polynesians began to arrive on Maui's shores about AD 800. They had journeyed from the Marquesas and Society Islands and braved rough waters in their canoes as they navigated by the stars across thousands of miles. These first residents brought animals, such as pigs and chickens, as well as plants, such as breadfruit, yams, coconuts, and bananas.

Not until 1778 did the Mauians receive their first visitor, when Captain James Cook made his second voyage to the Hawaiian Islands. Months earlier, Cook had landed on Kauai and Niihau; he had made friends with the Polynesians and left behind bartered goods, as well as dreaded white-man's diseases. When he got to Maui, Cook was surprised to find that the venereal disease running rampant on his ships had preceded him there. Shortly after, Cook pushed on to the Big Island.

Before leaving, however, Cook anchored his ship off the northeast coast of Maui while he hosted Kalaniopuu, the aging chief of the Big Island, who spent a night on the Englishman's HMS *Resolution*. At the time, the Hawaiian Islands were rife with divided kingdoms waging war one against another, and the elderly Kalaniopuu was certainly plotting against Maui's principal chief, Kahekili. How much Cook figured into these strategy sessions is unknown, but the records show that Kalaniopuu was accompanied by his young warrior nephew, Kamehameha.

Perhaps it was the experience off Maui's coast that eventually fired Kamehameha's ambition to rule more than a tiny section of one island. Kamehameha witnessed that Cook was master of his destiny, and the callow youth, no doubt, wanted the same thing. Years of battle followed as the young chief fought for the right to dominate the Islands. Finally, in 1794, Kamehameha defeated Maui's chief, thereby gaining the Valley Isle as well as its smaller neighboring islands of Molokai and Lanai. The following year, he conquered the Big Island and Oahu. Kauai wouldn't knuckle under, but in 1810 it was won over diplomatically. Kamehameha had earned the right to be king of all the islands. He was called Kamehameha I, or Kamehameha the Great, and the kingdom's headquarters were in Lahaina, on Maui. To this day, you can see the remains of the king's Lahaina palace between the Pioneer Inn and the ocean.

The great king had 21 wives during his lifetime, and the two most notable hailed from Maui. Queen Keopuolani was Kamehameha's "sacred" wife, the daughter of a traditional brother-sister union that was considered so powerful that Keopuolani was assured of producing honorable heirs for her husband. Historians believe she was the first Christian convert; she was extremely supportive of the missionaries who came to Hawaii. Preceded in death by her royal spouse, Queen Keopuolani is buried in the Wainee/Waiola Cemetery (on Wainee Street in Lahaina), next to her second husband, Hawaiian chief Hoapili, who was governor of Maui.

Kamehameha's favorite wife, Kaahumanu, also came from Maui. She was tall, statuesque, and politically astute. In fact, after her husband's death in 1819, Queen Kaahumanu named herself Hawaii's first regent when Keopuolani's eldest son, Liholiho, took the throne; she even continued that role when Liholiho's brother Kauikeaouli succeeded him. Kaahumanu was so powerful that she was instrumental in banning the *kapu* system, the Hawaiian set of rules and standards that had been in force for generations. It was she who insisted that the king move from the Brick Palace in Lahaina to another home in Honolulu.

Not long after Captain Cook landed on Maui, others arrived to take up residence. Missionaries who came from the eastern United States thought Mauians were heathens who needed to be saved, and they tried diligently to convert the residents. The missionaries' job was made even more challenging by the almost simultaneous arrival of whalers from New England. Soon Lahaina developed into the area's most important whaling port, and with the new industry came a lusty lifestyle that included more diseases, wild revelry, and additional motivation for the missionaries to continue their quest.

In 1840, King Kamehameha III moved his monarchic capital to Honolulu, but Lahaina continued to be an important city for trade, education, and hearty living. Many of the buildings used during this era still exist in Lahaina and are open to visitors. The Spring House now located in the Wharf Shopping Center on Front Street once protected a freshwater source for the missionaries, while the Seamen's Hospital, also on Front Street, was converted by the U.S. government from a royal party residence to a medical facility for sailors.

Along with missionaries and whalers, other new settlers started to come to Maui. The most notable arrivals were businessmen, who viewed the Islands as a place to buy cheap land—or, better yet, to get it for free by befriending a member of the royal family. To the most astute entrepreneurs, sugar, which grew wild on Maui, looked like a good bet for cultivation, and when the Civil War knocked out sugar supplies in the South, the Hawaiian plantations boomed. By the late 1800s, "King Sugar" had become the new ruler in the Islands.

Some of the most prominent leaders in the sugar industry were the grown children of missionaries. On Maui two of the most important businessmen were Samuel Alexander and Henry Baldwin, who joined forces in a sugar dynasty eventually called Alexander & Baldwin. A&B, as it came to be known, was a charter member of Hawaii's Big Five—the five giant corporations that controlled the Islands economically and politically well into the 20th century. Although the power and influence of the Big Five have waned dramatically in the past five years with the increase of takeovers and buy-outs, Alexander & Baldwin remains Maui's largest private landholder and largest private employer. The company developed the sunny Wailea Resort and owned it until last year, as well as all of the island's sugar operations and macadamia-nut farms.

It wasn't until the early 1960s—only a few years after Hawaii became a state in 1959—that tourism took root on Maui in a major way. That was when Amfac Inc., the largest of the Big Five, opened its major resort destination in West Maui, calling it Kaanapali. It soon became Hawaii's second most popular resort area after Waikiki and was the first to boast a master plan. The Royal Lahaina, which opened in 1962, was the first lodging to break ground in the Kaanapali Resort, which now contains six hotels and six condominiums. The resort's once-scruffy 3-mile beach area has been spruced up so that it now is a sophisticated blend of active night spots, rambling golf greens, fine restaurants, and free-form pools.

North of Kaanapali, Maui Land & Pineapple entered into the tourism arena in the mid-1970s when it broke ground on the Kapalua Resort with its 194-room Kapalua Bay Hotel. (Incidentally, Maui Land & Pineapple, like Alexander & Baldwin, is still partly owned by missionaries' descendants.) In Wailea, on Maui's south shore, Alexander & Baldwin, in partnership with the mainland-based Northwestern Mutual Life Insurance, introduced its Wailea Resort, in 1975. During the following decade, the companies put up two hotels and three condominium projects. Four more hotels at the resort have either just opened or will open within the next two years.

Tourism now accounts for about half of all jobs on the Valley Isle. Beginning in the mid-1800s, the dwindling indigenous population—those Hawaiians whose descendants came from the Marquesas and the Society Islands—were reinforced by labor from Japan, China, Portugal, and the Philippines, so that today's Maui has become a melting pot of ethnicity and culture.

The Valley Isle is full of people ready to share the friendly aloha spirit. If you take the drive to Hana, down hundreds of hairpin curves, across bridges, and past waterfalls, you'll find a gentle folk who still speak the Hawaiian language. On a stroll through the streets of Wailuku, you'll meet elderly Filipino men who can remember their parents' stories of the old country. Or if you relax on the wharf in historic Lahaina, you can watch transplanted Californians have a great time surfing—most of them find West Maui the best place in the world to work and live. All these residents love their island and will gladly help you have a good time.

By all means, make the effort. Although a fantastic time can be had simply by bronzing on the silky-soft, white-sand beaches, the wonder of Maui is that much, much more awaits your discovery. Don't be surprised if quite a few of your fantasies are actually fulfilled. The Valley Isle hates to let anyone down.

1 Essential Information

Before You Go

Visitor Information

A trip is a considerable investment in both time and money, and a travel agent who has been to Hawaii can help you cut through a lot of the details. He or she will also know most of the airline packages and special tours. Most travel agents work on a commission from the airlines, hotels, and attractions. You pay no more—and often less—than if you made your arrangements on your own.

For free brochures and other general information relating to Maui and the state of Hawaii, contact the **Hawaii Visitors Bureau** (HVB) office nearest you:

New York: 441 Lexington Ave., Suite 1003, NY 10017, tel. 212/986–9203.
Chicago: 180 N. Michigan Ave., Suite 1031, IL 60601, tel. 312/236–0632.
San Francisco: 50 California St., Suite 450, CA 94111, tel. 415/392–8173.
Los Angeles: 3440 Wilshire Blvd., Suite 502, CA 90010, tel. 213/385–5301.
Great Britain: c/o First Public Relations Ltd., 2 Cinnamon Row, Plantation Wharf, York Place, London SW11 3TW, tel. 071/924–3999.

You may also contact HVB offices in Hawaii:

Oahu (main office): Waikiki Business Plaza, 2270 Kalakaua Ave., Suite 801, Honolulu, HI 96815, tel. 808/923–1811.
Maui: 111 Hana Hwy., Suite 112, Kahului, HI 96732, tel. 808/871–8691.

Hawaii Visitors Bureau publishes three free booklets. The *Calendar of Events* lists all the special holidays and annual festivals in the state of Hawaii. The *Accommodation Guide* covers various lodging choices in Hawaii, in every price range, with information on amenities. HVB's *Restaurant Guide* lists the 560 HVB-member restaurants throughout the state with one-line descriptions and price categories.

Tour Groups

Package tours to Hawaii usually include airfare, accommodations, transfers, some sightseeing, and plenty of free time for the beach. Choosing a tour comes down to how inclusive you want it to be: Do you want to know all your meals are paid for before you leave, or would you rather hunt out a local eatery? Would you prefer to arrange a private sail, or is a group outing on a catamaran fine with you?

When considering a tour, be sure to find out (1) exactly what expenses are included—particularly tips, taxes, side trips, additional meals, and entertainment; (2) ratings of all hotels on the itinerary and the facilities they offer; (3) cancellation policies for both you and the tour operator; (4) the number of travelers in your group; and (5) if you are traveling alone, the cost of the single supplement. Note whether the tour operator reserves the right to change hotels, routes, or even prices after you've booked, and check out the operator's policy regarding cancellations, complaints, and trip-interruption insurance. Most tour operators request that bookings be made through a travel agent—in most cases there is no additional charge for doing so.

General-Interest Tours   **Maupintour** (Box 807, Lawrence, KS 66044, tel. 913/843–1211 or 800/255–4266) combines Oahu with Maui, Kauai, and the Big Island of Hawaii in various itineraries. A 13-day trip to all of the larger four islands includes helicopter "flightseeing." **American Express Vacations** (Box 5014, Atlanta, GA 30302, tel. 800/241–1700) and **Pleasant Hawaiian Holidays** (2404 Townsgate Rd., Westlake Village, CA 91361, tel. 818/991–3390 or 800/2–HAWAII) are veritable supermarkets of tours, offering both escorted and independent packages. Other major operators include **Cartan Tours** (2809 Butterfield Rd., Oak Brook, IL 60521, tel. 800/422–7826, 708/571–1400, or 800/422–7826), **Tauck Tours** (11 Wilton Rd., Westport, CT 06881, tel. 203/226–6911 or 800/468–2825), and **Trieloff Tours** (24031 El Toro Rd., Laguna Hills, CA 92653, tel. 714/855–2126 or 800/248–6877).

Special-Interest Tours
Adventure   **Sobek Expeditions** (Box 1089, Angels Camp, CA 95222, tel. 209/736–4524) offers an off-the-beaten-track camping trip to Maui, Kauai, and the Big Island.

Conservation   **The Sierra Club** (730 Polk St., San Francisco, CA 94109, tel. 415/776–2211) spreads its conservation message by taking people on-site to see for themselves why an area should be preserved. Trips vary from year to year, but a wide array is offered. Call for more information.

Natural History   **Questers Worldwide Nature Tours** (257 Park Ave. S, New York, NY 10010, tel. 212/673–3120) hikes into undeveloped areas throughout the islands to study native plant and animal life, volcanoes, and other exceptional settings.

British Tour Operators   **Albany Travel (Manchester) Ltd.** (Central Buildings, 211 Deansgate, Manchester M2 5QR, tel. 061/833–0202) offers packages from seven nights or more, with an option to combine stays on several islands.
Kuoni Travel Ltd. (Kuoni House, Dorking, Surrey RH5 4AZ, tel. 0306/76711) offers beach holidays on Waikiki Beach and Maui. A stopover in Los Angeles is also available.
Sovereign Holidays (Groundstar House, London Rd., Crawley, W. Sussex RH10 2TB, tel. 0293/561444).

Package Deals for Independent Travelers

U.S. Tour Operators   **American Express Vacations** and **Pleasant Hawaiian Holidays** (*see* General-Interest Tours, above) both offer catalogues full of air/hotel packages. **GoGo Tours** (69 Spring St., Ramsey, NJ 07446, tel. 201/934–3500 or 800/821–3731) has packages ranging from 2 to 16 days with options for sightseeing and discount car rental. **Classic Hawaii** (1 N. 1st St., San Jose, CA 95113, tel. 408/287–9101 or 800/221–3949) features the Islands' more upscale hotels and resorts. Also check with **TWA Getaway Vacations** (tel. 800/GETAWAY), **American Fly AAway Vacations** (tel. 800/443–7300), **Continental Grand Destinations** (tel. 713/821–2100 or 800/634–5555), **Delta Airlines** (tel. 404/765–2952 or 800/241–6108), and **United Vacations** (tel. 312/952–4000 or 800/328–6877).

Passports, Visas, and Customs

Travel Documents Persons who are not citizens of the United States require a passport and a visa. Canadians only need to prove their place of birth, with a passport, birth certificate, or similar document. British travelers will need a valid, 10-year passport (cost £15) and a U.S. Visitor's Visa, which you can get either through your travel agent or by post from the **United States Embassy, Visa and Immigration Dept.** (5 Upper Grosvenor St., London W1A 2JB, tel. 071/499–3443 for a recorded message, or 071/499–7010). The embassy no longer accepts visa applications made by personal callers. No vaccinations are required.

Restrictions on Import and Export Plants and plant products are subject to control by the Department of Agriculture, both on entering and leaving Hawaii. Pineapples and coconuts pass freely; papayas must be treated. All other fruits are banned for export to the U.S. mainland. Flowers pass except for gardenia, rose leaves, jade vine, and mauna loa. Seeds, except in leis and jewelry, are banned. Also banned are insects, snails, coffee, cotton, cacti, sugarcane, all berries, and soil.

Customs for British Travelers If you are 21 or over, you may take into the United States 200 cigarettes or 50 cigars or 2 kilograms of tobacco; one liter of alcohol; and duty-free gifts to a value of $100. Be careful not to try to take in meat or meat products, seeds, plants, or fruits. Avoid illegal drugs like the plague.

Returning to the United Kingdom you may take home, if you are 17 and over: (1) 200 cigarettes or 100 cigarillos or 50 cigars or 250 grams of tobacco; (2) two liters of table wine and (a) one liter of alcohol over 22% by volume (most spirits), or (b) two liters of alcohol under 22% by volume (fortified or sparkling wine) or (c) two more liters of table wine; (3) 60 milliliters of perfume and 250 milliliters of toilet water; and (4) other goods up to a value of £32, but not more than 50 liters of beer or 25 cigarette lighters.

Pets Leave dogs and other pets at home. A strict 120-day quarantine is imposed to keep out rabies, which is nonexistent in Hawaii. For full details, write to the **Animal Quarantine Station, Department of Agriculture,** State of Hawaii, 99–770 Moanalua Rd., Aiea, HI 96701.

When to Go

A few years back, Hawaii narrowly missed its chance to be voted the country's best place to live. The reason? The climate was too perfect. Although Upcountry Maui temperatures can drop to as low as 40°F on a chilly night and standing at the peak of Haleakala is almost always a downright frigid experience, Maui's balmy weather is a boon to year-round vacationing.

Remember, too, this rule of island climatology: The mountains in the island's center stop the rain clouds, which tend to move east to west. These conditions create a wet, cooler climate on the eastern side of the island and leave the western side hot and dry. You'll find the best weather in the West Maui destinations of Kaanapali and Kapalua and Central Maui's Wailea Resort. Temperatures year-round at the beaches average about 75°F; Upcountry is about 10° cooler. East Maui gets more than 70 inches of rain in an average year; West Maui gets no more than 15.

The island's peak tourist seasons fall between December 15 and Easter and during the summer. At these times, Maui will be more crowded and more expensive. You'll find escalated prices especially in the midwinter season.

Climate The following are average maximum and minimum temperatures for certain areas of Maui:

Hana

Jan.	79F	26C	**May**	81F	27C	**Sept.**	85F	29C
	63	17		65	18		68	20
Feb.	79F	26C	**June**	83F	28C	**Oct.**	83F	28C
	63	17		67	19		67	19
Mar.	79F	26C	**July**	83F	28C	**Nov.**	81F	27C
	63	17		67	19		67	19
Apr.	79F	26C	**Aug.**	83F	28C	**Dec.**	79F	26C
	65	18		68	20		65	18

Kaanapali

Jan.	79F	26C	**May**	81F	27C	**Sept.**	85F	29C
	65	18		67	19		70	21
Feb.	77F	25C	**June**	83F	28C	**Oct.**	85F	29C
	63	17		68	20		70	21
Mar.	79F	26C	**July**	85F	29C	**Nov.**	83F	28C
	67	19		72	22		68	20
Apr.	81F	27C	**Aug.**	85F	29C	**Dec.**	79F	26C
	65	18		72	22		67	19

Lahaina

Jan.	85F	29C	**May**	86F	30C	**Sept.**	88F	31C
	61	16		63	17		70	21
Feb.	83F	28C	**June**	88F	31C	**Oct.**	88F	31C
	59	15		65	18		68	20
Mar.	85F	29C	**July**	88F	31C	**Nov.**	86F	30C
	63	17		65	18		67	19
Apr.	85F	29C	**Aug.**	88F	31C	**Dec.**	83F	28C
	63	17		68	20		65	18

Updated hourly weather information in over 750 cities around the world—450 of them in the United States—is only a phone call away. Dialing WeatherTrak at 900/370–8728 will connect you to a computer, with which you can communicate by touch tone—at a cost of 75¢ for the first minute and 50¢ each minute thereafter. A taped message will tell you to dial the three-digit access code to any of the 750 cities. The code is either the area code (in the United States) or the first three letters of the foreign city. For a list of all access codes, send a stamped, self-addressed envelope to Cities, Box 7000, Dallas, TX 75209. For further information, phone 800/247–3282.

A similar service operated by American Express can be accessed by dialing 900/WEATHER (900/932–8437). As well as supplying a three-day weather forecast for 600 cities worldwide, this service provides international travel information and time and day. The cost is 75¢ per minute.

Festivals and Seasonal Events

For further information contact the Hawaii Visitors Bureau (*see* Visitor Information, above).

Feb.–March: Cherry Blossom Festival. This popular celebration of all things Japanese includes a run, cultural displays, cooking demonstrations, music, and the inevitable queen pageant and coronation ball.

Mar. 26: Prince Kuhio Day. The state holiday honors Prince Kuhio, a man who might have been a king if Hawaii had not been granted statehood. Instead the man became a respected congressman.

Apr.: Art Maui. The best of a wide variety of media is shown at this prestigious annual event.

Apr.: Buddha Day. Flower pageants are staged at temples to celebrate the birth of Buddha.

May 1: Lei Day. The annual flower-filled celebration includes music, hula, food, as well as lots of leis on exhibit and for sale, some of them exquisite floral masterpieces.

May: Barrio Festival. This cultural celebration is organized by the Binha Filipino Community.

May: Junior World Wave Sailing Championships. Competitors under age 18 come from 15 countries to race the challenging surf at Hookipa Beach.

June: King Kamehameha Day. Kamehameha united all the islands to become Hawaii's first king (and making Hawaii the only state to have a royal background). Festivities include parades and fairs.

July: Makawao Statewide Rodeo. This old-time Upcountry rodeo, held at the Oskie Rice Arena, includes the annual Makawao Rodeo Parade.

July 4: Independence Day. The national holiday is celebrated with a tropical touch, including fairs, parades, and, of course, fireworks. Special events include the Great Kalua Pig Cook-Off in Maui, with a $1,000 cash prize for the best pig roaster in the state, a pig parade, and good eating.

Aug. 18: Admission Day. The local holiday recognizes Hawaii's statehood.

Sept.–Oct.: Aloha Week Festival. This traditional celebration, started in 1946, preserves Hawaiian native culture. Crafts, music, dance, pageantry, street parties, and canoe races highlight the festival.

Nov.: Maui Classic NCAA Basketball Tournament. The collegiate competition is held at the Lahaina Civic Center.

Nov.: Kapalua International Championship Golf. Top pro golfers meet at the Kapalua resort for the "Super Bowl" of golf with a purse of over $600,000.

Nov.: Na Mele O'Maui Festival. Hawaiian arts, crafts, dances, music, and a luau are all part of this cultural event.

Dec.: Bodhi Day. The traditional Buddhist Day of Enlightenment is celebrated at temples throughout the island. Visitors are welcome at the services.

Dec. 25: Christmas. The hotels outdo one another in extravagant exhibits and events, such as Santa arriving by outrigger canoe.

What to Pack

You can pack lightly because Maui is casual. Bare feet, bathing suits, and comfortable, informal clothing are the norm.

The Man's Suitcase In the Hawaiian Islands, there's a saying that when a man wears a suit during the day, he's either going for a loan or he's a lawyer trying a case. Only a few upscale restaurants require a jacket for dinner, and none requires a tie. Maui regulars wear their jackets on the plane—just in case—and many don't put them on again until the return flight. The aloha shirt is accepted dress in Maui for business and most social occasions. A visitor can easily buy one after arriving.

Shorts are acceptable daytime attire, along with a T-shirt or polo shirt. If you want to be marked as a tourist, wear your shorts with dark shoes and white socks. Local-style casual footwear consists of tennis or running shoes, sandals, or rubber slippers. You'll also see a lot of bare feet, but state law requires that footwear be worn in all food establishments.

Pack your toiletries, underwear, and a pair or two of easy-care slacks to wear with those aloha shirts, and you're all set.

Female Fashion During the winter months, be sure to bring a sweater or wrap for the evening because the trade winds cool things off as soon as the sun goes down. If you have an elaborate coiffure, a scarf will help keep it from getting windblown.

Sundresses, shorts, and tops are fine for daytime. During the summer months, synthetic slacks and shirts, although easy to care for, can get uncomfortably warm. If you have a long slip, bring it for the muumuu you say you won't buy, but probably will. As for shoes, sandals and tennis or running shoes are fine for daytime, and sandals are perfect for the evening. If you wear boots, you'll wish you hadn't.

If you don't own a *pareu*, buy one in Maui. It's simply a length (about 1½ yards long) of light cotton in a tropical motif that can be worn as a beach wrap, a skirt, or a dozen other wrap-up fashions. A pareu is useful wherever you go, regardless of climate. It makes a good bathrobe, so you don't have to pack one. You can even tie it up as a handbag or sit on it at the beach.

For Everyone Don't forget your bathing suit. Sooner or later, the crystal-clear water tempts even the most sedentary landlubber. Of course, bathing suits are easy to find in Maui. Shops are crammed with the latest styles. If you wear a bathing cap, bring one; you can waste hours searching for one.

Probably the most important thing to tuck in your suitcase is sunscreen. This is the tropics, and the ultraviolet rays are much more powerful than those to which you are accustomed. Doctors advise putting on sunscreen when you get up in the morning. Women can wear it as a moisturizer under makeup. The upper chest area of a woman is hypopigmented and should be protected. Don't forget to reapply sunscreen periodically during the day, since perspiration can wash it away. Consider using sunscreens with a sun protection factor (SPF) of 15 or higher. There are many tanning oils on the market in Maui, including coconut and kukui oils, but doctors warn that they merely sauté your skin. Too many Hawaiian vacations have been spoiled by sunburn.

Visitors who wear glasses are wise to pack an extra pair. Eyeglasses are easy to lose, and you can waste days of your precious Hawaiian holiday replacing them.

If you're planning to visit a volcano area, bring along a lightweight jacket, especially in the winter months.

It's a good idea to tuck in a few jumbo zip-lock plastic bags when you travel—they're ideal for wet swimsuits or food souvenirs that might leak. All hotels in Maui provide beach towels. Some hotels provide hair dryers and some don't. Unless you know for sure, bring your own.

Luggage
Carry-on Luggage

Passengers on U.S. airlines are limited to two carry-on bags. For a bag you wish to store under the seat, the maximum dimensions are 9″ × 14″ × 22″. For bags that can be hung in a closet or on a luggage rack, the maximum dimensions are 4″ × 23″ × 45″. For bags you wish to store in an overhead bin, the maximum dimensions are 10″ × 14″ × 36″. Any item that exceeds the specified dimensions may be rejected as a carryon and taken as checked baggage. Keep in mind that an airline can adapt the rules to circumstances, so on an especially crowded flight don't be surprised if you are allowed only one carry-on bag.

In addition to the two carryons, you may bring aboard a handbag (pocketbook or purse); an overcoat or wrap; an umbrella; a camera; a reasonable amount of reading material; an infant bag; and crutches, cane, braces, or other prosthetic device. An infant/child safety seat can also be brought aboard if parents have purchased a ticket for the child or if there is space in the cabin.

Foreign airlines have slightly different policies. They generally allow only one piece of carry-on luggage in tourist class, in addition to handbags and bags filled with duty-free goods. Passengers in first and business class are also allowed to carry on one garment bag. It is best to call your airline to find out its current policy.

Checked Luggage

U.S. airlines allow passengers to check in two suitcases whose total dimensions (length + width + height) do not exceed 62 inches and whose weight does not exceed 70 pounds.

Rules governing foreign airlines can vary, so check with your travel agent or the airline itself before you go. All airlines allow passengers to check in two bags. In general, expect the weight restriction on the two bags to be not more than 70 pounds each, and the size restrictions on the bags to be 62 inches total dimensions.

Cash Machines

Virtually all U.S. banks belong to a network of ATMs (Automatic Teller Machines), which gobble up bank cards and spit out cash 24 hours a day in cities throughout the country. There are eight major networks in the United States, the largest of which are Cirrus, owned by MasterCard, and Plus, affiliated with Visa. Some banks belong to more than one network. These cards are not automatically issued; you have to ask for them. If your bank doesn't belong to at least one network, you should consider moving your account, for ATMs are becoming as essential as check cashing. Cards issued by Visa, MasterCard, and American Express may also be used in the ATMs, but the fees are usually higher than the fees on bank cards (and there is a daily interest charge on the "loan," even if monthly bills are paid on time). Each network has a toll-free number you can call to locate machines in a given city. The Cirrus number is 800/4–CIRRUS; the Plus number is 800/THE–PLUS. Check with your bank for fees and for the amount of cash you can withdraw on any given day; also ask for a list of banks in Hawaii that will honor your bank cash card.

Car Rentals

During peak seasons—summer and Christmas through Easter—be sure to reserve your car well ahead of time. Although you'll generally pay a higher price in the peak seasons, you'll find Maui one of the cheapest U.S. destinations for renting an auto. Expect to pay about $35 a day for a compact car from one of the major companies. You can get an even more inexpensive deal from one of the locally owned budget companies. For these, you'll probably have to call for a shuttle from the airport since they often don't have rental desks there.

Before you leave home, find out if your hotel and air package includes a car—many packages do, and the deals offered by tour wholesalers are often less than the prices you'll find when you arrive in Maui. Airlines such as Hawaiian Airlines and Aloha Airlines often provide car tie-ins with a lower than normal rate. On fly/drive deals, ask whether the car-rental company will honor a reservation rate if it must upgrade you to a larger vehicle upon arrival.

Before calling or arriving in person at the rental desk, do a bit of homework to save yourself some money. Check with your personal or business insurance agent to see if your coverage already includes rental cars. Signing up for the collision damage waiver (CDW) offered by the rental agency quickly inflates that "What-a-deal" rate before you ever leave the parking lot. Some credit card companies also offer rental-car coverage.

When booking over the phone, be certain to ask whether you're responsible for additional mileage and for returning the car with a full fuel tank, even if you don't use all the gas. In addition, be sure to get a confirmation number for your car reservation, and check to see if the rental company offers unlimited mileage and a flat rate per day, which are definite advantages. Last but not least, check beforehand on the credit cards honored by the company.

When you get your rental car, be sure to ask for a *Maui Drive Guide*, which provides detailed maps for the entire island. The roads in Maui are basically simple to follow, and as long as you stay on the pavement, they're safe as well. Most rental-car companies forbid driving *off* the pavement, so if you elect to do this, you're taking a big chance.

Budget (tel. 800/527–0707), **Dollar** (tel. 800/367–7006), and **National** (tel. 800/CAR–RENT) have desks at the Kapulua–West Maui Airport, while **Hertz** (tel. 800/654–3131), **Alamo** (tel. 800/327–0633), **Thrifty** (tel. 800/367–2277) and **Tropical** (tel. 800/367–5140) are nearby. All the above, plus **Avis** (tel. 800/331–1212), **Robert's** (tel. 808/947–3939), and **United** (tel. 800/657–7797), have desks at or near Maui's major airport in Kahului. In addition, quite a few locally owned companies rent cars on Maui, including **Rent-A-Jeep** (tel. 808/877–6626), **Payless Car Rental** (tel. 800/345–5230), and **Trans-Maui** (tel. 800/367–5228). They are near the Kahului Airport and will pick you up only from there.

Insurance

Travelers may seek insurance coverage in three areas: health and accident, loss of luggage, and trip cancellation. Your first step is to review your existing health and homeowner policies; some health insurance plans cover health expenses incurred while traveling, some major medical plans cover emergency transportation, and some homeowner policies cover the theft of luggage.

Health and Accident Several companies offer coverage designed to supplement existing health insurance for travelers:

Carefree Travel Insurance (Box 310, 120 Mineola Blvd., Mineola, NY 11501, tel. 516/294–0220 or 800/323–3149) provides coverage for emergency medical evacuation and accidental death and dismemberment. It also offers 24-hour medical phone advice.

International SOS Assistance (Box 11568, Philadelphia, PA 19116, tel. 215/244–1500 or 800/523–8930), a medical assistance company, provides emergency evacuation services, worldwide medical referrals, and optional medical insurance.

Travel Guard International, Transamerica Occidental Life Companies (1145 Clark St., Stevens Point, WI 54481, tel. 715/345–0505 or 800/782–5151), offers reimbursement for medical expenses, with no deductibles or daily limits, and emergency evacuation services.

Wallach and Company, Inc. (243 Church St. NW, Suite 100D, Vienna, VA 22180, tel. 703/281–9500 or 800/237–6615), offers comprehensive medical coverage, including emergency evacuation services worldwide.

British Travelers We recommend that to cover health and motoring mishaps, you insure yourself with **Europ Assistance** (252 High St., Croydon, Surrey CRO INF, tel. 081/680–1234).

Lost Luggage The loss of luggage is usually covered as part of a comprehensive travel insurance package that includes personal accident, trip cancellation, and sometimes default and bankruptcy insurance. Several companies offer comprehensive policies:

Access America Inc., a subsidiary of Blue Cross-Blue Shield (Box 11188, Richmond, VA 23230, tel. 800/334–7525 or 800/284–8300).

Near Services, 450 Prairie Ave., Suite 101, Calumet City, IL 60409, tel. 708/868–6700 or 800/654–6700).

Travel Guard International (*see* Health and Accident Insurance, above).

Trip Cancellation Flight insurance is often included in the price of a ticket when paid for with American Express, Visa, and other major credit and charge cards. It is usually included in combination travel insurance packages available from most tour operators, travel agents, and insurance agents.

British Travelers   **The Association of British Insurers** (Aldermary House, 10–15 Queen St., London EC4N 1TT, tel. 071/248–4477) will give comprehensive advice on all aspects of vacation insurance.

Traveling with Film

If your camera is new, shoot and develop a few rolls before leaving home. Pack some lens tissue and an extra battery for your built-in light meter. Invest about $10 in a skylight filter and screw it onto the front of your lens. It will protect the lens and also reduce haze.

Film doesn't like hot weather. If you're driving in summer, don't store film in the glove compartment or on the shelf under the rear window. Put it behind the front seat on the floor, on the side opposite from the exhaust pipe.

On a plane trip, never pack unprocessed film in check-in luggage; if your bags get X-rayed, you can say good-bye to your pictures. Always carry undeveloped film with you through security, and ask to have it inspected by hand. (It helps to isolate your film in a plastic bag, ready for quick inspection.) Inspectors at American airports are required by law to honor requests for hand inspection; abroad, you'll have to depend on the kindness of strangers.

The old airport scanning machines—still in use in some countries—use heavy doses of radiation that can turn a family portrait into an early morning fog. The newer models—used in all U.S. airports—are safe for anything from five to 500 scans, depending on the speed of your film. The effects are cumulative; you can put the same roll of film through several scans without worry. After five scans, though, you're asking for trouble.

If your film gets fogged and you want an explanation, send it to the National Association of Photographic Manufacturers (550 Mamaroneck Ave., Harrison, NY 10528). It will try to determine what went wrong. The service is free.

Traveling with Children

Publications   ***Family Travel Times*** is an 8- to 12-page newsletter published 10 times a year by TWYCH (Travel with Your Children, 80 8th Ave., New York, NY 10011, tel. 212/206–0688). A one-year subscription costs $35 and includes access to back issues and twice-weekly opportunities to call in for specific information. Send $1 for a sample issue.

Great Vacations with Your Kids, by Dorothy Jordon (founder of TWYCH) and Marjorie Cohen, offers complete advice on planning a trip with children (toddlers to teens) and details everything from city vacations to adventure vacations to childcare resources. If unavailable from your local bookseller, it can be ordered from E. P. Dutton, 2 Park Ave., New York, NY 10016, tel. 212/725–1818.

Kids and Teens in Flight is a Department of Transportation brochure with information on young people traveling alone. To order free copies, call 202/366–2220.

Getting There   On domestic flights, children under two not occupying a seat travel free. Various discounts apply to children two to 12 years of age. Regulations about infant travel on airplanes are in the

process of changing. Until they do, however, if you want to be
sure your infant is secured in his/her own safety seat, you must
buy a separate ticket and bring your own infant car seat.
(Check with the airline in advance; certain seats aren't allowed.
Or write for the booklet *Child/Infant Safety Seats Acceptable
for Use in Aircraft,* from the Federal Aviation Administration,
APA–200, 800 Independence Ave., SW, Washington, DC
20591, tel. 202/267–3479.) Some airlines allow babies to travel
in their own safety seats at no charge if there's a spare seat on
the plane available, otherwise safety seats will be stored and
the child will have to be held by a parent. If you opt to hold your
baby on your lap, do so with the infant outside the seatbelt so
he or she won't be crushed in case of a sudden stop.

Also inquire about special children's meals or snacks. See the
February 1990 or 1992 issue of *Family Travel Times* for
"TWYCH's Airline Guide," which contains a rundown of the
children's services offered by 46 airlines.

Hints for Disabled Travelers

In Hawaii The Society for the Advancement of Travel for the Handicapped has named Hawaii the most accessible vacation spot for
the disabled; the number of ramped visitor areas and specially
equipped lodgings in the state attests to its desire to make
everyone feel welcome. Several agencies and companies make
helping the disabled their number one priority. **The Commission on Persons with Disabilities** (5 Waterfront Plaza, Suite 210,
500 Ala Moana Blvd., Honolulu 96813) offers information con-
cerning accessibility on the Islands; it also publishes helpful
travelers' guides that list support services on the Islands for
disabled visitors.

Those who prefer to do their own driving may rent hand-con-
trolled cars from **Avis** (tel. 800/831–8000), which suggests a
one-month advance reservation. **Hertz** (tel. 800/654–3131) also
rents left- or right-hand controlled cars at no additional
charge. A two-day notice is required, and an additional $25 de-
posit is required from customers renting on a cash basis.

Additional **The Information Center for Individuals with Disabilities** (Fort
Information Point Pl., 1st floor, 27-43 Wormwood St., Boston, MA 02210,
tel. 617/727–5540; TDD 617/727–5236) offers useful problem-
solving assistance, including lists of travel agents who special-
ize in tours for the disabled.

Moss Rehabilitation Hospital Travel Information Service (1200
W. Tabor Rd., Philadelphia, PA 19141, tel. 215/456–9600; TDD
215/456–9602) provides information on tourist sights, transportation, and accommodations in destinations around the
world. The fee is $5 for up to three destinations. Allow one
month for delivery.

Mobility International USA (Box 3551, Eugene, OR 97403, tel.
503/343–1284) is a membership organization with a $20 annual
fee offering information on accommodations, organized study,
and so forth around the world.

The National Park Service provides a **Golden Access Passport**
free of charge to those who are blind or who have a permanent
disability; the passport covers the entry fee for the holder and
anyone accompanying the holder in the same private, noncommercial vehicle and a 50% discount on camping, boat launching,

and parking. All charges are covered except lodging. Apply for the passport in person at any national recreation facility that charges an entrance fee; proof of disability is required. For additional information, write to the National Park Service (Box 37127, Washington, DC 20013).

The Society for the Advancement of Travel for the Handicapped (26 Court St., Penthouse Suite, Brooklyn, NY 11242, tel. 718/858–5483) offers access information. Annual membership costs $45, $25 for senior travelers and students. Send $1 and a stamped, self-addressed envelope.

Travel Industry and Disabled Exchange (TIDE, 5435 Donna Ave., Tarzana, CA 91356, tel. 818/368–5648) is an industry-based organization with a $15 per person annual membership fee. Members receive a quarterly newsletter and information on travel agencies and tours.

Publications *Access America: An Atlas and Guide to the National Parks for Visitors with Disabilities* (published by Northern Cartographic, Box 133, Burlington, VT 05402, tel. 802/860–2886) contains detailed information about access for the 37 largest and most visited national parks in the United States. It costs $40 plus $5 shipping.

Access to the World: A Travel Guide for the Handicapped, by Louise Weiss. If unavailable from your local bookseller, it can be ordered from Henry Holt & Co. (tel. 800/247–3912; the order number is 0805 001417) for $12.95 plus $2 shipping and handling.

Hints for Older Travelers

The American Association of Retired Persons (AARP, 1909 K St. NW, Washington, DC 20049, tel. 202/872–4700) has two programs for independent travelers: (1) The Purchase Privilege Program, which offers discounts on hotels, airfare, car rentals, and sightseeing; and (2) the AARP Motoring Plan, provided by Amoco, which furnishes emergency aid (road service) and trip-routing information for an annual fee of $33.95 per couple. AARP members must be at least 50 years old. Annual dues are $5 per person or per couple.

To use an AARP or other identification card, ask for a reduced hotel rate at the time you make your reservation, not when you check out. At participating restaurants, show your card to the maître d' before you're seated, since discounts may be limited to certain set menus, days, or hours. Your AARP card will identify you as a retired person but will not ensure a discount in all restaurants. When renting a car, be sure to ask about special promotional rates, which may offer greater savings than that available with your ID card.

Elderhostel (75 Federal St., 3rd floor, Boston, MA 02110–1914, tel. 617/426–7788) is an innovative program for people age 60 or over (only one member of a traveling couple needs to qualify). Participants live in dormitories on some 1,200 campuses in the United States and around the world. Mornings are devoted to lectures and seminars, afternoons to sightseeing and field trips. The fee for a trip includes room, board, tuition (in the United States and Canada) and round-trip transportation (overseas). Special scholarships are available for those who qualify financially in the United States and Canada.

The Golden Age Passport is a free lifetime pass to all parks, monuments, and recreation areas run by the federal government. Permanent U.S. residents age 62 and over may pick them up in person at any of the national parks that charge admission. Proof of age is necessary. The passport covers the entrance fee for the holder and anyone accompanying the holder in the same private (noncommercial) vehicle. It also provides a 50% discount on camping, boat launching, and parking (lodging is not included). For additional information, contact the National Park Service (Box 37127, Washington, DC 20013).

Greyhound/Trailways (tel. 800/752–4841) offers special fares for senior citizens; the rates are subject to date and destination restrictions. **Amtrak** (tel. 800/USA–RAIL) requests 48 hours notice to provide redcap service, special seats, or wheelchair assistance at stations equipped to provide this service.

Mature Outlook (6001 N. Clark St., Chicago, IL 60660, tel. 800/336–6330), a subsidiary of Sears, Roebuck & Co., is a travel club for people over 50 years of age, offering Holiday Inn discounts and a bimonthly newsletter. Annual membership is $9.95 per couple.

National Council of Senior Citizens (925 15th St. NW, Washington, DC 20005, tel. 202/347–8800) is a nonprofit advocacy group with some 5,000 local clubs across the country. Annual membership is $12 per person or per couple. Members receive a monthly newspaper with travel information and an ID for reduced-rate hotels and car rentals.

September Days Club (tel. 800/241–5050) is run by the moderately priced Days Inns of America. The $12 annual membership fee for individuals or couples over 50 entitles them to reduced car rental rates and reductions of 15%–50% at 95% of the chain's more than 350 motels.

Publications   *The Discount Guide for Travelers over 55,* by Caroline and Walter Weintz, lists helpful addresses, package tours, reduced-rate car rentals, etc., in the United States and abroad. If unavailable at your local bookstore, send $7.95, plus $1.50 shipping and handling, to NAL/Cash Sales (Bergenfield Order Dept., 120 Woodbine St., Bergenfield, NJ 07621, tel. 800/526–0275). Include ISBN 0–525–48358–6.

The International Health Guide for Senior Citizen Travelers, by W. Robert Lange, MD, is available for $4.95, and *The Senior Citizens Guide to Budget Travel in the United States and Canada,* by Paige Palmer, is available for $3.95, plus $1 for shipping from Pilot Books (103 Cooper St., Babylon, NY 11702, tel. 516/422–2225).

Further Reading

Before your trip, pick up a copy of James Michener's *Hawaii,* one of the best novels set in the Hawaiian Islands. Other excellent novels with a Hawaiian setting include James Jones's *From Here to Eternity* and John Dominis Holt's *Waimea Summer,* based on the author's experiences growing up in Hawaii.

To find out more about Hawaiian history, try Gavan Daws's definitive *Shoal of Time,* which will take you from Captain Cook's landing until statehood in 1959. *Maui, How It Came to Be,* by Will Kyselka, will tell you more about Maui's origins. *Maui,*

Mischievous Hero, by Barbara Lyons, illuminates the legends of the Valley Isle. Mary Kawena Pukui's *Place Names of Hawaii* can tell you how some of the interesting names in the state originated.

Rita Ariyoshi's *Maui on My Mind* is a beautiful collection of photographs in a coffee-table-book format as is *A Day in the Life of Hawaii. Hawaiian Hiking Trails*, by Craig Chisholm, gives a good idea of the best paths to take around Maui. John R. K. Clark's *The Beaches of Maui County* offers a good overview of the island's surf and sand. *Pidgin to Da Max*, by Douglas Simonson, explains the humorous Pidgin English you'll no doubt hear all over the Hawaiian Islands.

Maui's art-focused *Pacific Art & Travel* magazine is available once you arrive on the Valley Isle or by contacting Pacific Islands Publishing (891 Eha St., Wailuku 96793, tel. 808/244–8844). Maui's other magazines include the general-interest *Maui Quarterly*, published by the Maui Visitors Bureau (380 Dairy Rd., Kahului 96733, tel. 808/871–8691), and the business-oriented *Maui, Inc., Magazine* (Box 425, Kahului 96732, tel. 808/244–7500).

Arriving and Departing

By Plane

Booking your Hawaii flight will be easy because a number of major airlines regularly service the destination. If, however, you are traveling from anywhere other than a West Coast city, you should know the distinction among the types of flights available. The quickest way to get from your home to a Hawaiian beach is to catch a nonstop flight from one of the country's major gateway cities. On direct flights you stay on the same aircraft, but make one or more stops; connecting flights involve one or more plane changes at one or more stops. If you can tolerate the plane-hopping, connecting flights are often the least expensive way to go.

Airports   Hawaii's major airport is **Honolulu International** (tel. 808/836–6411), about a five-hour flight from West Coast cities and a 20-minute drive from Waikiki. Unless you're taking a nonstop flight from the West Coast to Maui, your plane will make a stop at this airport. The facility currently is undergoing major renovation that makes it more cumbersome to navigate now, but this should ease congestion when work is finished in 1993. The Honolulu Airport is packed with shops perfect for last-minute buying: places where you can get a lei, a pineapple, T-shirts, and even Gucci bags. If you're flying from Honolulu to Maui, you'll need to locate one of the two separate interisland terminals to the left of the main terminal as you exit. A complimentary Wiki Wiki Shuttle will take you to and from the interisland terminals; however, it's an easy five-minute walk between the international and the interisland terminals.

Maui's major airport, in Kahului, at the center of the island, is currently undergoing a $100 million, 10-year renovation, which began in 1982. Its new terminal opened in late 1990 and was still ironing out a few rough spots at press time. Still, **Kahului Airport** (tel. 808/877–6431), is efficient and easy to navigate. Its major disadvantage is its distance from the major resort destinations in West Maui and Wailea. It will take you about an hour, with traffic in your favor, to get to a hotel in West Maui and about 20 to 30 minutes to go to Wailea. However, Kahului is the only airport on Maui that has direct service from the mainland.

If you're staying in West Maui, you might be better off flying into the new **Kapalua–West Maui Airport** (tel. 808/669–0228), an $8.5 million facility that opened in 1987. The only way to get to the Kapalua–West Maui Airport is on an interisland flight, however, since the short runway allows only small planes to land there. The little airport is set in the midst of a pineapple field with a terrific view of the ocean far below and provides one of the most pleasant ways to arrive on the Valley Isle. It was built by a locally based carrier, Hawaiian Air, which years ago had purchased small planes, giving it exclusive rights in West Maui. Before long, however, competitor Aloha Airlines figured out a way to fly into the Kapalua facility: It simply purchased commuter carrier Princeville Airways—which already flew the requisite-size prop planes—and renamed it Aloha IslandAir. Several major rental-car companies have desks right inside the terminal. Shuttles also run between the airport and the Kaanapali and Kapalua resorts.

The only other airport on Maui is **Hana Airport** (tel. 808/248–8208), which is not much more than a landing strip. Only commuter Aloha IslandAir flies there, landing about once an hour. When there is no flight, the tiny terminal usually stands eerily empty, with no gate agents, ticket takers, or other people in sight. If you are staying at the Hotel Hana-Maui, your flight will be met; if you have reserved a rental car, the agent will usually know your arrival time and meet you. Otherwise you can call **Dollar Rent A Car** to pick you up (tel. 808/248–8237).

Flights from North America **United Airlines** (tel. 800/241–6522) flies directly to Kahului from Los Angeles, Chicago, and San Francisco while **American Airlines** (tel. 800/433–7300) also flies into Kahului, with one stop in Honolulu, from Los Angeles, Chicago, Detroit, Houston, St. Louis, New York, and Dallas. **Delta** (tel. 800/221–1212) has through service to Maui daily from Salt Lake City, Atlanta, Dallas, and Los Angeles.

Maui is part of the world's most isolated chains of islands, so even if you fly directly to the Valley Isle, be prepared for a lengthy flight. From the West coast, Maui is about 5 hours; from the Midwest, expect about an 8-hour flight; and coming from the East coast will take about 10 hours. If you have to connect with an interisland flight in Honolulu, add at least another hour.

Maui is two hours behind Los Angeles, three hours behind Salt Lake City, four hours behind Chicago, and five hours behind New York. Hawaii doesn't turn back its clocks for daylight savings time, however, so add an extra hour to the time difference during the summer.

Flights from Honolulu In addition, **Continental** (tel. 800/525–0280), **Hawaiian** (tel. 800/367–5320), **Northwest** (tel. 800/225–2525), **America West** (tel. 800/247–5692), **Pan Am** (tel. 800/221–1111), and **TWA** (tel. 800/221–2000) fly from the mainland to Honolulu, where Maui-bound passengers can connect with a 20- to 30-minute interisland flight. Interisland flights generally run about $50 one-way between Honolulu and Maui and are available many times each day from **Hawaiian Airlines** (tel. 800/367–5320), **Aloha Airlines** (tel. 800/367–5250), and **Aloha IslandAir** (tel. 800/323–3345). In fact, Maui is the most visited of the Neighbor Islands and therefore the easiest to connect to on an interisland flight. Flying a commuter carrier like Aloha IslandAir can take a few minutes longer, since the planes are generally small prop planes. Flights on all carriers usually stop running around 8 PM and begin again at about 6:30 the next morning.

Flights from Great Britain Airlines flying to Maui include **British Airways, TWA, Pan Am, Aer Lingus, American Airlines** and **Northwest Airlines.**

If you can afford to be flexible about when you travel, look for last-minute flight bargains and other flight advertisements in magazines (such as *Time Out*) and the Sunday papers.

Thomas Cook Ltd. can often book you on very inexpensive flights. Ring the Cook branch nearest you and ask to be put through to the "Airfare Warehouse." Be sure to ring at least 21 days in advance of when you want to travel.

Trailfinders (42–48 Earl's Court Rd., Kensington, London W8 6EJ, tel. 071/937–5400) can arrange flights to Honolulu.

Other International Flights Foreign air carriers are prohibited by law from serving Hawaii from American cities. Should your travel plans bring you from other parts of the world, however, **Canadian Airlines** (tel. 800/426–7000), **Qantas** (tel. 800/227–4500), **Air New Zealand** (tel. 800/521–4059), **China Airlines** (tel. 808/536–6951), and **Japan Airlines** (tel. 800/525–3663), among others, fly to Honolulu.

Discount Flights Charter flights from the mainland United States are the least expensive way to fly, but you pay a price in reliability. Sometimes they're late, sometimes they cancel. They also depart less frequently than regularly scheduled flights—usually about once a week. If the savings seem worth it, you'll still have to negotiate an interisland fare to Maui, since these charter companies serve only Honolulu International Airport. Try **Air America** (tel. 808/833–4433 or 800/247–2475) or **Trans Air** (tel. 808/833–5557). Some tour wholesalers and airlines also occasionally run a charter. For more information on charters, ask your travel agent.

Between the Airport and Your Destination
By Bus/Shuttle If you're staying at the Kaanapali Beach Resort and fly into the Kapalua–West Maui Airport, you can take advantage of the resort's free shuttle and go back to the airport later to pick up your car. During daylight hours, the shuttle passes through the airport at regular intervals. Likewise, a **Gray Line-Maui** bus (tel. 808/877–5507) operates between Kahului and Kaanapali every hour between 7 AM and 5 PM. If you book the Hotel Hana-Maui, the charge for pickup at Hana Airport is included in the rate.

By Taxi You could also opt for a taxi. Maui has more than two dozen taxi companies, and they make frequent passes through the airport. If you don't see a cab, you can call **Yellow Cab** (tel. 808/877–7000) or **La Bella Taxi** (tel. 808/242–8011) for islandwide service from the airport, or **Kihei Taxi** (tel. 808/879–3000) if you're staying in the Kihei, Wailea, or Makena areas. Charges from Kahului Airport to Kaanapali run about $35; to Wailea, about $20; and to Lahaina, about $30.

By Car Frankly, the best way to get from the airport to your destination is in your own rental car. You're going to need it for the rest of the trip; you might as well get it right away. Most major car-rental companies have conveniently located desks at each airport (*see* Car Rentals in Before You Go, above).

Lei Greeting For some visitors, it's a rude awakening to get off a plane in Hawaii with no lei to greet them. Some arrangement needs to be made in advance should you want such a welcome. If you've purchased a package that includes a lei greeting, rest assured, there'll be a lei waiting for you. If friends are meeting you at the airport, they'll also know the island custom. If you're traveling independently, however, you can still receive a lei upon arrival by asking your travel agent to make arrangements with one of several companies. **Greeters of Hawaii** (Box 29638, Honolulu 96820, tel. 800/367–2669) operates statewide. **Airport Flower & Fruit** (460 Dairy Rd., Kahului 96732, tel. 800/922–9352), based on Maui, also does a good job.

By Ship

When Pan Am's amphibious *Hawaii Clipper* touched down on Pearl Harbor's waters in 1936 it marked the beginning of the end of regular passenger ship travel to the Islands. From that point on, the predominant means of transporting visitors would be by air, not by sea. Today, however, cruising to Hawaii still holds a special appeal for those with the time and money to afford sailing, and with a bit of work, you can arrange passage aboard the luxury liners that call on Honolulu when traveling the Seven Seas.

No regularly scheduled American ships steam between the Mainland and Hawaii. Although foreign-owned vessels often ply the Pacific, the Jones Act of 1896 prohibits them from carrying passengers between two U.S. ports unless the ships first stop at an intervening foreign port or carry the passengers to a foreign destination. What that means to those wishing for the relaxing ways of ship travel is that they'll have to book with one of the major lines passing through Honolulu. For details, check with such lines as **Cunard/N.A.C. Line, Holland American Line,** and **Royal Viking** (tel. vary from city to city).

From Honolulu Approaching the Valley Isle from the deck of a ship is a great orientation. Watching the land loom ever larger conjures up the same kinds of feelings the early Polynesians probably had on their first voyage—except they didn't get the kind of lavish treatment those on board a luxury cruise ship routinely receive. If this is an option that appeals to you, you can book passage through **American Hawaii Cruises** (550 Kearny St., San Francisco, CA 94108, tel. 800/765–7000), which offers seven-day interisland cruises departing from Honolulu on the SS *Constitution* and the SS *Independence*. Both have recently been renovated.

Staying in Maui

Getting Around

By Car Maui, the second-largest island in the state of Hawaii, with 729
Driving square miles, has some 120 miles of coastline, not all of which is accessible. Less than one-quarter of its land mass is inhabited.

To see the island your best bet is a car, because there is no reliable public transportation.

Maui has several major roads. Highway 30, or the Honoapiilani Highway, goes from Wailuku in Central Maui around the south of the West Maui mountains and up past Lahaina, Kaanapali, and Kapalua. The road from the Kahului Airport to Kihei, Wailea, and Makena is called Highway 350, or the Mokulele Highway. When you reach Kihei, you can take Kihei Road to reach all the lodgings in that town, or you can bypass them on Highway 31 (the Piilani Highway) if you're staying in Wailea or Makena. The latter road is the best on the island in terms of driving because it is wide and sparsely traveled. Another main thoroughfare is Highway 37, or the Haleakala Highway, which goes between Kahului and Haleakala. Most of the island's roads have two lanes.

If you're going to attempt the dirt roads between Kapalua and Wailuku or from Hana to Makena, you'll need a four-wheel-drive vehicle, but be forewarned: Rental-car companies prohibit travel off the pavement, so if you break down, you're on your own for repairs. The only other difficult road on Maui is Highway 36, or the Hana Highway, which runs 56 miles between Kahului and Hana and includes more twists and turns than a person can count. Take it slow and you should have no problems.

Car Rentals   *See* Car Rentals in Before You Go, above.

By Shuttle   If you're staying in the right hotel or condo, there are a few shuttles that can get you around the area. The **Kaanapali–Lahaina Shuttle** runs daily from the Royal Lahaina Hotel in Kaanapali to the Wharf Shopping Center in Lahaina every half hour between 8 AM and 10:25 PM with stops at all Kaanapali hotels. The cost is $1.50. The **Kaanapali Shuttle** runs within the resort between 7 AM and 11 PM and stops automatically at all hotels and at condos when requested. It also goes to and from Lahaina at 55-minute intervals. It's free. All Kaanapali hotels have copies of schedules, or you can call the Kaanapali Beach Operators Association (tel. 808/661–3271). The free **Aston Hotels Shuttle** in the Kaanapali area runs from 8 AM to 6 PM for guests who want to go to the Whalers Village Shopping Center and Lahaina. You can get schedules at Aston hotel desks. The **Wailea Shuttle** and the **Kapalua Shuttle** run within their respective resorts and are free; schedules are available throughout each resort.

By Taxi   For short hops between hotels and restaurants, this can be a convenient way to go, but you'll have to call ahead. Even busy West Maui doesn't have curbside taxi service. **West Maui Taxi** (761 Kumukahi, Lahaina, tel. 808/667–2605) and **Yellow Cab of Maui** (Kahului Airport, tel. 808/877–7000) both service the entire island, but you'd be smart to consider using them just for the areas where they're located. **Alii Cab** (475 Kuai Pl., Lahaina, tel. 808/661–3688) specializes in West Maui, while **Kihei Taxi** (Kihei, tel. 808/879–3000) serves Central Maui.

By Limousine   **Arthur's Limousine Service** (Box 11865, Lahaina 96761, tel. 800/345–4667) provides a chauffeured superstretch Lincoln complete with two TVs, three bars, and two sunroofs for $60 per hour. **Inlanda Inc.** (91 Alo Alo Pl., Lahaina 96761, tel. 808/669–7800) has Cadillacs and Lincolns from $48 an hour. Both companies are based in or near Lahaina but serve the entire island. There's a minimum time requirement—usually two hours—

but the companies have put together personalized sightseeing tours just to make it easy for you.

By Moped/ Mopeds from **A&B Moped Rental** (3481 Lower Honoapiilani
Motorcycle Hwy., Lahaina, tel. 808/669–0027) go for about $25. You can
get bicycles at AA Go Go for $10 to $20. Be especially careful
navigating the roads on Maui, since there are no designated bicycle or moped lanes.

Important Addresses and Numbers

Tourist **Maui Visitors Bureau** (380 Dairy Rd., Kahului 96732, in
Information Kahului's industrial district, tel. 808/871–8691).
Maui Chamber of Commerce (26 Puunene Ave., Kahului 96732,
also in the industrial district, tel. 808/871–7711).

Emergencies **Police, fire,** or **ambulance** (tel. 911).

Doctors **Doctors on Call** (Hyatt Regency Maui-Napili Tower #1,
Kaanapali, tel. 808/667–7676) and **Maui Physicians** (3600 Lower
Honoapiilani Rd., Lahaina, tel. 808/669–9600) are doctors
serving West Maui. Another walk-in clinic at Whalers Village,
West Maui Healthcare Center (2435 Kaanapali Pkwy., Suite
H-7, Kaanapali, tel. 808/667–9721) also serves West Maui. Created by two doctors in 1980 to treat tourists, the clinic is open
daily 7 AM–11 PM. **Kihei Clinic** and **Wailea Medical Services**
(1993 S. Kihei Rd., Kihei, tel. 808/879–1440 or 808/879–7447)
are based in the more central part of the Valley Isle. All of the
above groups are geared toward working with visitors.

Hospitals **Hana Medical Center** (Hana Hwy., Hana, tel. 808/248–8294).

Kula Hospital (204 Kula Hwy., Kula, tel. 808/878–1221).

Maui Memorial Hospital (221 Mahalani, Wailuku, tel. 808/244–
9056).

Pharmacies Maui has no 24-hour pharmacies but several where you can get
prescriptions filled during daylight hours. The least expensive
are the island's two **Longs Drug Stores** (Maui Mall, corner of
Kaahumanu and Puunene Aves., Kahului, tel. 808/877–0068;
Lahaina Cannery Shopping Center, Honoapiilani Hwy., tel.
808/667–4390; both open daily, 8:30 AM–9 PM). **Kihei Drug** is in
the Kihei Town Center (1881 S. Kihei Rd., Kihei, tel. 808/879–
1915; open weekdays 8:30–7, Saturday 8:30–5:30, Sunday
10–3).

Road Service On Maui, the one **AAA** garage that offers 24-hour islandwide
service is **Sunset Towing** (Bldg. 30, Halawai Rd., Kaanapali,
tel. 808/667–7048). It specializes in serving West Maui and
Kahului but will travel anywhere on Maui with a tow truck.

Grocers Three major groceries are open 24 hours a day. **Safeway,** at the
Lahaina Cannery Shopping Center (Honoapiilani Hwy.,
Lahaina, tel. 808/667–4392), serves West Maui, while **Food-
land,** in the Kihei Town Center (1881 S. Kihei Rd., Kihei, tel.
808/879–9350) and Safeway (170 E. Kam Ave., tel. 808/877–
3377) operate on the island's other side.

Weather **National Weather Service/Maui Forecast** (tel. 808/877–5111).
Haleakala Weather Forecast (tel. 808/871–5054).

Others **Coast Guard Rescue Center** (tel. 808/244–5256).

Suicide and Crisis Center Help Line (tel. 808/244–7407).

Opening and Closing Times

Banks on the island are generally open Monday–Thursday 8:30–3, Friday 8:30–6.

Shops are generally open seven days a week, 9–5. Shopping centers tend to stay open later (until 9 on certain days).

Guided Tours

If getting yourself oriented on an island doesn't come easy, try taking one of a variety of guided tours offered on Maui. This is a perfect opportunity to benefit from the services of an expert who can point out the sights you're most interested in and explain what it all means. Basically, you have your choice of getting oriented from the ground or from the air.

By Land **Circle Island Tour.** This is a big island to tour in one day, so several companies combine various sections of it—either Haleakala, Iao Needle, and Central Maui, or West Maui and its environs. Some stops include the historical sections of the county seat of Wailuku, while others focus on some of the best snorkeling spots. Call a selection of companies to find the tour that suits you. The cost is usually $35–$65 for adults, half that for children.

Haleakala Sunrise Tour. This tour starts before dawn so that visitors get a chance to actually make it to the top of the dormant volcano before the sun peeks over the horizon. Some companies throw in champagne to greet the sunrise. Cost of the six-hour tour: about $45.

Haleakala/Upcountry Tour. Usually a half-day excursion, this tour is offered in several versions by different companies. The trip often includes stops at a protea farm and at Tedeschi Vineyards and Winery, the only place in Hawaii where wine is made. Cost: about $40 adults, $20 children.

Hana Tour. This tour is almost always done in a van, as the winding road to Hana just doesn't provide a comfortable ride in bigger buses. Of late, Hana has so many of these one-day tours that it seems as if there are more vans than cars on the road. Still, it's a more relaxing way to do the drive than behind the wheel of your own car. Guides decide where you stop for photos. Cost: about $60.

Tour Companies Ground-tour companies are usually statewide and have a whole fleet of vehicles. Some use air-conditioned buses, while others prefer smaller vans. Then you've got your minivans, your microbuses, and your minicoaches. The key is how many passengers each will hold. Be sure to ask how many stops you'll get on your tour, or you may be disappointed to find that all your sightseeing is done through a window.

Most of the tour guides have been in the business for years; some were born in the Islands and have taken special classes to learn more about their culture and lore. They expect a tip ($1 per person at least), but they're just as cordial without one.

There are many ground-tour companies. Here are some of the most reliable and popular ones, with their mailing addresses:

Akamai Tours (Box 395, Kahului 96732, tel. 800/922–6485) does a good job, and it's always recognizable by its bright yellow vans.

Gray Line Hawaii (273 Dairy Rd., Kahului 96732, tel. 800/367–

2420 or 808/877–5507) uses air-conditioned motor coaches, limos, and vans.

No Ka Oi Scenic Tours (Box 1827, Kahului 96732, tel. 808/871–9008) specializes in a Hana tour.

Maui Fun Centers (2191 S. Kihei Rd., Kihei 96753, tel. 808/874–3773) offers van, bicycle, and hiking tours.

Polynesian Adventure Tours (536 Keolani Pl., Kahului 96732, tel. 800/622–3011 or 808/877–4242) has guides that keep up an amusing patter. The talk can get annoying, however, if you're more interested in the serious stuff.

Roberts Hawaii Tours (Box 247, Kahului 96732, tel. 808/871–6226) and **Trans Hawaiian Services** (3111 Castle St., Honolulu 96815, tel. 800/533–8765) are two of the largest companies in the state, but each manages to keep its tours personal.

By Air   **Circle Island Tour.** Helicopter companies handle this in different ways. Some have fancy names, such as Ultimate Experience or Circle Island Deluxe. Some go for two hours or more. Cost: about $185–$200.

Hana/Haleakala Crater Tour. This takes about 90 minutes to travel inside the volcano, then down to the Hawaiian village of Hana. Some companies stop in secluded areas for refreshments, but local residents have had moderate success in getting this stopped. Cost: about $130.

West Maui Tour. Generally a 30-minute helicopter ride over Kaanapali and Lahaina. Frankly, this is not a very exciting helicopter tour. Cost: about $70–$95.

Tour Companies   About seven helicopter companies regularly offer air tours over Maui. If you're at all nervous, ask about the company's safety record, although most are reliable. The best Maui operators include **Hawaii Helicopters** (Kahului Heliport, Hangar 106, Kahului 96732, tel. 808/877–3900 or 800/346–2403 from the Mainland), **Maui Helicopters** (Box 1002, Kihei 96753, tel. 808/879–1601 or 800/367–8003 from the Mainland), **Papillon Hawaiian Helicopters** (Box 1478, Kahului 96732, tel. 808/669–4884 or 800/367–7095), and **Kenai Helicopters** (Box 685, Puunene 96784, tel. 808/871–6483 or 800/622–3144).

Special-Interest   Once you have your bearings, you may want a tour that's a bit
Tours   more specialized. For example, you may have a hankering for hunting but not know where to go. You might want to bike down a volcano or visit artists. Here are some tours to meet those needs:

Haleakala Downhills. It started back in 1983 with **Cruiser Bob's Original Haleakala Downhill** (99 Hana Hwy., Box B, Paia 96779, tel. 808/579–8444), which now has competition from **Maui Downhill Bicycle Safaris** (199 Dairy Rd., Kahului 96732, tel. 800/535–2453) and **Maui Mountain Cruisers** (Box 1356, Makawao 96768, tel. 800/232–MAUI). All three companies will put you on a bicycle at the top of Haleakala and let you coast down. Safety precautions are top priority, so riders wear helmets and receive training in appropriate bicycle-bell ringing. Meals are provided. Cost: $85–$100.

Hiking Tours. Hike Maui (Box 330969, Kahului 96733, tel. 808/879–5270) is owned by naturalist Ken Schmitt, who guides some 50 different hikes himself. Prices range from $60 for a 4-mile, five-hour hike to $990 for a week-long trek with accommodations and all meals. **Maui-Anne's Island Photography Tours** (Box 2250, Kihei 96753, tel. 808/874–3797) offers hiking trips with a focus on photography. A wide variety of tours and prices is available upon request.

Horseback Tours. At least two companies on Maui now offer horseback riding that's far more appealing than the typical hour-long trudge over a boring trail with 50 other horses. Mauian Frank Levinson started **Adventures on Horseback** (Box 1771, Makawao 96768, tel. 808/242–7445) a few years back with five-hour outings into secluded parts of Maui. The tours traverse ocean cliffs on Maui's north shore, along the slopes of Haleakala, as they pass by streams, through rain forests, and near waterfalls. The $125-per-person price includes breakfast, lunch, and refreshments. **Charley's Trail Rides & Pack Trips** (c/o Kaupo Store, Kaupo 96713, tel. 808/248–8209) requires an even more stout physical nature, as the overnighters go from Kaupo—a *tiny* village nearly 20 miles past Hana—up the slopes of Haleakala to the crater. For parties of four to six, the per-person charge is $150, including meals and cabin or campsite equipment, or $125 without meals. Charges are higher for fewer people.

Hunting Adventures of Maui (645-B Kaupakalua Rd., Haiku 96708, tel. 808/572–8214). This is a guided excursion on more than 100,000 acres of private ranch land on Maui, a "fair chase" hunt for Spanish mountain goats and wild boar. Maui has a year-round hunting season, so this tour is always available. Cost: $400 for the first person, $200 for each additional hunter. Cost includes transportation, food, beverages, clothing, boots, packs, and meat storage and packing for shipping. Nonhunters can accompany the tour free.

Maui Art Tours (Box 1058, Makawao 96768, tel. 808/572–7132). Maui publisher Barbara Glassman produces a book every year that catalogues and pictures Maui artists and their work in exchange for an entry fee. That project has been successful, so Glassman now offers a tour that takes creative types into artists' homes for tea and conversation. Limo transportation and an elegant lunch are provided, as is the opportunity to buy art directly from the artists. This is a very enjoyable, refined tour that costs $150. Maui Art Tours will customize each tour, letting clients choose the type of art they want to see and even how many artists they want to visit.

Star-gazing. Take a star-studded trip with **Astronomy Tours Maui** (1597 Aa St., Lahaina 96761, tel. 808/667–9080). An astronomer leads this tour to Haleakala's summit to view the sunset and stars. Dinner at Kula Lodge is included in the $85 package; $50 for children 12 and under.

Personal Guides **Local Guides of Maui** (333 Dairy Rd., Kahului 96732, tel. 800/228–6284). This is *the* best way to see Maui through the eyes of the locals. Started by Laurie Robello, who is part-Hawaiian, the company now has more than a dozen guides. Your guide will come to your hotel, but then transportation is in your car, which he or she will drive. Local Guides of Maui tailors its tours to your particular interests—one elderly lady wanted to meet senior citizens who live on Maui, and that's exactly what she got to do. Others just want to sample life Hawaiian-style, so Local Guides of Maui takes them to the secret swimming holes, the hidden hot spots, and even home to meet the family. Local Guides of Maui charges $165 for two people all day; each additional person is $20.

Temptation Tours (RR1, Box 454, Kula 96790, tel. 808/877–8888). At the other end of the spectrum is this company, which leads you around luxuriously. Company president Dave Campbell has targeted members of the affluent older crowd (though almost anyone would enjoy these tours) who don't want to be herded into a crowded bus. He provides exclusive tours in his plush, six-passenger limo-van and specializes in full-day tours to Haleakala and Hana. The "Hana Ultimate" includes a lunch at the Hotel Hana-Maui. You can also choose to include a helicopter ride. Prices vary depending on the degree of customization; the average Hana tour, with a picnic lunch, however, runs about $105, plus tax, per person.

Walking Tours   The **Lahaina Restoration Foundation** (Baldwin Home, 696 Front St., Lahaina, tel. 808/661–3262) has published a walking-tour map for interested visitors. The map will guide you past the most historic sites of Lahaina, some renovated and some not. Highlights of the walk include the Jodo Mission, the Brig *Carthaginian II*, The Baldwin Home, and the old Court House. These are all sights you could find yourself, but the map is free, and it makes the walk easier.

Credit Cards

The following credit card abbreviations are used: AE, American Express; DC, Diners Club; MC, MasterCard; V, Visa.

2 Portraits of Maui

The House of the Sun

Although it was written in the early 20th century, before Haleakala became a popular tourist attraction, Jack London's account of camping among the crater's cinder cones is still fascinating to read today.

by Jack London

There are hosts of people who journey like restless spirits round and about this earth in search of seascapes and landscapes and the wonders and beauties of nature. They overrun Europe in armies; they can be met in droves and herds in Florida and the West Indies, at the pyramids, and on the slopes and summits of the Canadian and American Rockies; but in the House of the Sun they are as rare as live and wriggling dinosaurs. Haleakala is the Hawaiian name for "the House of the Sun." It is a noble dwelling situated on the island of Maui; but so few tourists have ever peeped into it, much less entered it, that their number may be practically reckoned as zero. Yet I venture to state that for natural beauty and wonder the nature lover may see dissimilar things as great as Haleakala, but no greater, while he will never see elsewhere anything more beautiful or wonderful. Honolulu is six days' steaming from San Francisco; Maui is a night's run on the steamer from Honolulu, and six hours more, if he is in a hurry, can bring the traveler to Kolikoli, which is ten thousand and thirty-two feet above the sea and which stands hard by the entrance portal to the House of the Sun. Yet the tourist comes not, and Haleakala sleeps on in lonely and unseen grandeur.

Not being tourists, we of the *Snark* went to Haleakala. On the slopes of that monster mountain there is a cattle ranch of some fifty thousand acres, where we spent the night at an altitude of two thousand feet. The next morning it was boots and saddles, and with cowboys and pack horses we climbed to Ukulele, a mountain ranch house, the altitude of which, fifty-five hundred feet, gives a severely temperate climate, compelling blankets at night and a roaring fireplace in the living room. Ukulele, by the way, is the Hawaiian for "jumping flea," as it is also the Hawaiian for a certain musical instrument that may be likened to a young guitar. It is my opinion that the mountain ranch house was named after the young guitar. We were not in a hurry, and we spent the day at Ukulele, learnedly discussing altitudes and barometers and shaking our particular barometer whenever anyone's argument stood in need of demonstration. Our barometer was the most graciously acquiescent instrument I have ever seen. Also, we gathered mountain raspberries, large as hen's eggs and larger, gazed up the pasture-covered lava slopes to the summit of Haleakala, forty-five hundred feet above us, and looked down upon a mighty battle of the clouds that was being fought beneath us, ourselves in the bright sunshine.

Every day and every day this unending battle goes on. Ukiukiu is the name of the trade wind that comes raging down out of the northeast and hurls itself upon Haleakala. Now Haleakala is so bulky and tall that it turns the northeast trade wind aside on either hand, so that in the lee of Haleakala no trade wind blows at all. On the contrary, the wind blows in the counter direction, in the teeth of the northeast trade. This wind is called Naulu. And day and night and always Ukiukiu and Naulu strive with each other, advancing, retreating, flanking, curving, curling, and turning and twisting, the conflict made visible by the cloud masses plucked from the heavens and hurled back and forth in squadrons, battalions, armies, and great mountain ranges. Once in a while, Ukiukiu, in mighty gusts, flings immense cloud masses clear over the summit of Haleakala; whereupon Naulu craftily captures them, lines them up in new battle formation, and with them smites back at his ancient and eternal antagonist. Then Ukiukiu sends a great cloud army around the eastern side of the mountain. It is a flanking movement, well executed. But Naulu, from his lair on the leeward side, gathers the flanking army in, pulling and twisting and dragging it, hammering it into shape, and sends it charging back against Ukiukiu around the western side of the mountain. And all the while, above and below the main battlefield, high up the slopes toward the sea, Ukiukiu and Naulu are continually sending out little wisps of cloud, in ragged skirmish line, that creep and crawl over the ground, among the trees and through the canyons, and that spring upon and capture one another in sudden ambuscades and sorties. And sometimes Ukiukiu or Naulu, abruptly sending out a heavy charging column, captures the ragged little skirmishers or drives them skyward, turning over and over, in vertical whirls, thousands of feet in the air.

But it is on the western slopes of Haleakala that the main battle goes on. Here Naulu masses his heaviest formation and wins his greatest victories. Ukiukiu grows weak toward late afternoon, which is the way of all trade winds, and is driven backward by Naulu. Naulu's generalship is excellent. All day he has been gathering and packing away immense reserves. As the afternoon draws on, he welds them into a solid column, sharp-pointed, miles in length, a mile in width, and hundreds of feet thick. This column he slowly thrusts forward into the broad battle front of Ukiukiu, and slowly and surely Ukiukiu, weakening fast, is split asunder. But it is not all bloodless. At times Ukiukiu struggles wildly, and with fresh accessions of strength from the limitless northeast smashes away half a mile at a time at Naulu's column and sweeps it off and away toward West Maui. Sometimes, when the two charging armies meet end-on, a tremendous perpendicular whirl results, the cloud masses, locked together, mounting thousands of feet into the air and turning over and over. A favorite device of Ukiukiu is to send a low, squat formation, densely packed, forward along the ground and under Naulu. When Ukiukiu is under, he proceeds to buck. Naulu's mighty middle gives to the blow and bends upward, but usually he turns the attacking column back upon itself and sets it milling. And all the while the ragged little skirmishers, stray and detached, sneak through the trees and canyons, crawl along and through the grass, and surprise one another with unexpected leaps and rushes; while above, far above, serene and lonely in the rays of the setting sun, Haleakala looks down upon the conflict. And so, the night. But in the morning, after the fashion of trade winds, Ukiukiu gathers strength and sends the hosts of Naulu rolling back in confusion and rout. And one day is like another day in the battle of the clouds, where Ukiukiu and Naulu strive eternally on the slopes of Haleakala.

Again in the morning, it was boots and saddles, cowboys and pack horses, and the climb to the top began. One pack horse carried twenty gallons of water, slung in five-gallon bags on either side; for water is precious and rare in the crater itself, in spite of the fact that several miles to the north and east of the crater rim more rain comes down than in any other place in the world. The way led upward across countless lava flows, without regard for trails, and never have I seen horses with such perfect footing as that of the thirteen that composed our outfit. They climbed or dropped down perpendicular places with the sureness and coolness of mountain goats, and never a horse fell or balked.

There is a familiar and strange illusion experienced by all who climb isolated mountains. The higher one climbs, the more of the earth's surface becomes visible, and the effect of this is that the horizon seems uphill from the observer. This illusion is especially notable on Haleakala, for the old volcano rises directly from the sea, without buttresses or connecting ranges. In consequence, as fast as we climbed up the grim slope of Haleakala, still faster did Haleakala, ourselves, and all about us sink down into the center of what appeared a profound abyss. Everywhere, far above us, towered the horizon. The ocean sloped down from the horizon to us. The higher we climbed, the deeper did we seem to sink down, the farther above us shone the horizon, and the steeper pitched the grade up to that horizontal line where sky and ocean met. It was weird and unreal, and vagrant thoughts of Simm's Hole and of the volcano through which Jules Verne journeyed to the center of the earth flitted through one's mind.

And then, when at last we reached the summit of that monster mountain, which summit was like the bottom of an inverted cone situated in the center of an awful cosmic pit, we found that we were at neither top nor bottom. Far above us was the heaven-towering horizon, and far beneath us, where the top of the mountain should have been, was a deeper deep, the great crater, the House of the Sun. Twenty-three miles around stretched the dizzy walls of the crater. We stood on the edge of the nearly vertical western wall, and the floor of the crater lay nearly half a mile beneath. This floor, broken by lava flows and cinder cones, was as red and fresh and uneroded as if it were but yesterday that the fires went out. The cinder cones, the smallest over four hundred feet in height and the largest over nine hundred, seemed no more than puny little sand hills, so mighty was the magnitude of the setting. Two gaps, thousands of feet deep, broke the rim of the crater, and through these Ukiukiu vainly strove to drive his fleecy herds of trade-wind clouds. As fast as they advanced through the gaps, the heat of the crater dissipated them into thin air, and though they advanced always, they got nowhere.

It was a scene of vast bleakness and desolation, stern, forbidding, fascinating. We gazed down upon a place of fire and earthquake. The tie-ribs of earth lay bare before us. It was a workshop of nature still cluttered with the raw beginnings of world-making. Here and there great dikes of primordial rock had thrust themselves up from the bowels of earth, straight through the molten surface ferment that had evidently cooled only the other day. It was all unreal and unbelievable. Looking upward, far above us (in reality beneath us) floated the cloud battle of Ukiukiu and Naulu. And higher up the slope of the seeming abyss, above the cloud battle, in the air and sky, hung the islands of Lanai and Molokai. Across the crater, to the southeast, still apparently looking upward, we saw ascending, first, the turquoise sea, then the white surf line of the shore of Hawaii; above that the belt of trade clouds, and next, eighty miles away, rearing their stupendous bulks out of the azure sky, tipped with snow, wreathed with cloud, trembling like a mirage, the peaks of Mauna Kea and Mauna Loa hung poised on the wall of heaven.

It is told that long ago, one Maui, the son of Hina, lived on what is now known as West Maui. His mother, Hina, employed her time in the making of kapas. She must have made them at night, for her days were occupied in trying to dry the kapas. Each morning, and all morning, she toiled at spreading them out in the sun. But no sooner were they out than she began taking them in, in order to have them all under shelter for the night. For know that the days were shorter then than now. Maui watched his mother's futile toil and felt sorry for her. He decided to do something—oh, no, not to help her hang out and take in the kapas. He was too clever for that. His idea was to make the sun go slower. Perhaps he was the first Hawaiian astronomer. At any rate, he took a series of observations of the sun from various parts of the island. His conclusion was that the sun's path was directly across Haleakala. Unlike Joshua, he stood in no need of divine assistance. He gathered a huge quantity of coconuts, from the fiber of which he braided a stout cord, and in one end of which he made a noose, even as the cowboys of Haleakala do to this day. Next he climbed into the House of the Sun and laid in wait. When the sun came tearing along the path, bent on completing its journey in the shortest time possible, the valiant youth threw his lariat around one of the sun's largest and strongest beams. He made the sun slow down some; also, he broke the beam short off. And he kept on roping and breaking off beams till the sun said it was willing to listen to reason. Maui set forth his terms of peace, which the sun accepted, agreeing to go more slowly thereafter. Wherefore Hina had ample time in which to dry her kapas, and the days are longer than they used to be, which last is quite in accord with the teachings of modern astronomy.

We had a lunch of jerked beef and hard poi in a stone corral, used of old time for the night impounding of cattle being driven across the island. Then we skirted the rim for half a mile and began the descent into the crater. Twenty-five hundred feet beneath lay the floor, and down a steep slope of loose volcanic cinders we dropped, the sure-footed horses slipping and sliding, but always keeping their feet. The black surface of the cinders, when broken by the horses' hoofs, turned to a yellow ocher dust, virulent in appearance and acid of taste, that arose in clouds. There was a gallop across a level stretch to the mouth of a convenient blowhole, and then the descent continued in clouds of volcanic dust, winding in and out among cinder cones, brick-red, old rose, and purplish black of color. Above us, higher and higher, towered the crater walls, while we journeyed on across innumerable lava flows, turning and twisting a devious way among the adamantine billows of a petrified sea. Saw-toothed waves of lava vexed the surface of this weird ocean, while on either hand rose jagged crests and spiracles of fantastic shape. Our way led on past a bottomless pit and along and over the main stream of the latest lava flow for seven miles.

At the lower end of the crater was our camping spot, in a small grove of olapa and kolea trees, tucked away in a corner of the crater at the base of walls that rose perpendicularly fifteen hundred feet. Here was pasturage for the horses, but no water, and first we turned aside and picked our way across a mile of lava to a known water hole in a crevice in the crater wall. The water hole was empty. But on climbing fifty feet up the crevice, a pool was found containing half a dozen barrels of water. A pail was carried up, and soon a steady stream of the precious liquid was running down the rock and filling the lower pool, while the cowboys below were busy fighting the horses back, for there was room for one only to drink at a time. Then it was on to camp at the foot of the wall, up which herds of wild goats scrambled and blatted, while the tent rose to the sound of rifle fir-

ing. Jerked beef, hard poi, and broiled kid was the menu.
Over the crest of the crater, just above our heads, rolled a
sea of clouds, driven on by Ukiukiu. Though this sea rolled
over the crest unceasingly, it never blotted out nor dimmed
the moon, for the heat of the crater dissolved the clouds as
fast as they rolled in. Through the moonlight, attracted by
the camp fire, came the crater cattle to peer and challenge.
They were rolling fat, though they rarely drank water, the
morning dew on the grass taking its place. It was because of
this dew that the tent made a welcome bedchamber, and we
fell asleep to the chanting of hulas by the unwearied Hawaiian cowboys, in whose veins, no doubt, ran the blood of
Maui, their valiant forebear.

The camera cannot do justice to the House of the Sun.
The sublimated chemistry of photography may not
lie, but it certainly does not tell all the truth. The
Koolau Gap [may be] faithfully reproduced, just as it im-
pinged on the retina of the camera, yet in the resulting picture the gigantic scale of things is missing. Those walls that
seem several hundred feet in height are almost as many
thousand; that entering wedge of cloud is a mile and a half
wide in the gap itself, while beyond the gap it is a veritable
ocean; and that foreground of cinder cone and volcanic ash,
mushy and colorless in appearance, is in truth gorgeous-
hued in brick-red, terra cotta, rose, yellow, ocher, and purplish black. Also, words are a vain thing and drive to
despair. To say that a crater wall is two thousand feet
high is to say just precisely that it is two thousand feet high;
but there is a vast deal more to that crater wall than a mere
statistic. The sun is ninety-three million miles distant, but
to mortal conception the adjoining county is farther away.
This frailty of the human brain is hard on the sun. It is likewise hard on the House of the Sun. Haleakala has a message
of beauty and wonder for the human soul that cannot be de-
livered by proxy. Kolikoli is six hours from Kahului;
Kahului is a night's run from Honolulu; Honolulu is six days
from San Francisco; and there you are.

We climbed the crater walls, put the horses over impossible
places, rolled stones, and shot wild goats. I did not get any
goats. I was too busy rolling stones. One spot in particular I
remember, where we started a stone the size of a horse. It
began the descent easy enough, rolling over, wobbling, and
threatening to stop; but in a few minutes it was soaring
through the air two hundred feet at a jump. It grew rapidly
smaller until it struck a slight slope of volcanic sand, over
which it darted like a startled jack rabbit, kicking up behind it a tiny trail of yellow dust. Stone and dust diminished
in size, until some of the party said the stone had stopped.
That was because they could not see it any longer. It had
vanished into the distance beyond their ken. Others saw it
rolling farther on—I know I did; and it is my firm conviction
that that stone is still rolling.

Our last day in the crater, Ukiukiu gave us a taste of his strength. He smashed Naulu back all along the line, filled the House of the Sun to overflowing with clouds, and drowned us out. Our rain gauge was a pint cup under a tiny hole in the tent. That last night of storm and rain filled the cup, and there was no way of measuring the water that spilled over into the blankets. With the rain gauge out of business there was no longer any reason for remaining; so we broke camp in the wet-gray of dawn and plunged eastward across the lava to the Kaupo Gap. East Maui is nothing more or less than the vast lava stream that flowed long ago through the Kaupo Gap; and down this stream we picked our way from an altitude of six thousand five hundred feet to the sea. This was a day's work in itself for the horses; but never were there such horses. Safe in the bad places, never rushing, never losing their heads, as soon as they found a trail wide and smooth enough to run on, they ran. There was no stopping them until the trail became bad again, and then they stopped of themselves. Continuously, for days, they had performed the hardest kind of work, and fed most of the time on grass foraged by themselves at night while we slept, and yet that day they covered twenty-eight leg-breaking miles and galloped into Hana like a bunch of colts. Also, there were several of them, reared in the dry region on the leeward side of Haleakala, that had never worn shoes in all their lives. Day after day, and all day long, unshod, they had traveled over the sharp lava, with the extra weight of a man on their backs, and their hoofs were in better condition than those of the shod horses.

The scenery between Vieiras's (where the Kaupo Gap empties into the sea) and Hana, which we covered in half a day, is well worth a week or a month; but, wildly beautiful as it is, it becomes pale and small in comparison with the wonderland that lies beyond the rubber plantations between Hana and the Honomanu Gulch. Two days were required to cover this marvelous stretch, which lies on the windward side of Haleakala. The people who dwell there call it "the ditch country," an unprepossessing name, but it has no other. Nobody else ever comes there. Nobody else knows anything about it. With the exception of a handful of men, whom business has brought there, nobody has heard of the ditch country of Maui. Now a ditch is a ditch, assumably muddy, and usually traversing uninteresting and monotonous landscapes. But the Nahiku Ditch is not an ordinary ditch. The windward side of Haleakala is serried by a thousand precipitous gorges, down which rush as many torrents, each torrent of which achieves a score of cascades and waterfalls before it reaches the sea. More rain comes down here than in any other region in the world. In 1904 the year's downpour was four hundred and twenty inches. Water means sugar, and sugar is the backbone of the territory of Hawaii, wherefore the Nahiku Ditch, which is not a ditch, but a chain of tunnels. The water travels underground, appearing only at intervals to leap a gorge, traveling high in the air on a giddy flume and plunging into and through the opposing mountain. This magnificent waterway is called a "ditch," and with equal appropriateness can Cleopatra's barge be called a boxcar.

There are no carriage roads through the ditch country, and before the ditch was built, or bored, rather, there was no horse trail. Hundreds of inches of rain annually, on fertile soil, under a tropic sun, means a steaming jungle of vegetation. A man, on foot, cutting his way through, might advance a mile a day, but at the end of a week he would be a wreck, and he would have to crawl hastily back if he wanted to get out before the vegetation overran the passageway he had cut. O'Shaughnessy was the daring engineer who conquered the jungle and the gorges, ran the ditch, and made the horse trail. He built enduringly, in concrete and masonry, and made one of the most remarkable water farms in the world. Every little runlet and dribble is harvested and conveyed by subterranean channels to the main ditch. But so heavily does it rain at times that countless spillways let the surplus escape to the sea.

The horse trail is not very wide. Like the engineer who built it, it dares anything. Where the ditch plunges through the mountain, it climbs over; and where the ditch leaps a gorge on a flume, the horse trail takes advantage of the ditch and crosses on top of the flume. That careless trail thinks nothing of traveling up or down the faces of precipices. It gouges its narrow way out of the wall, dodging around waterfalls or passing under them where they thunder down in white fury; while straight overhead the wall rises hundreds of feet, and straight beneath it sinks a thousand. And those marvelous mountain horses are as unconcerned as the trail. They fox-trot along it as a matter of course, though the footing is slippery with rain, and they will gallop with their hind feet slipping over the edge if you let them. I advise only those with steady nerves and cool heads to tackle the Nahiku Ditch trail. One of our cowboys was noted as the strongest and bravest on the big ranch. He had ridden mountain horses all his life on the rugged western slopes of Haleakala. He was first in the horse breaking; and when the others hung back, as a matter of course, he would go in to meet a wild bull in the cattle pen. He had a reputation. But he had never ridden over the Nahiku Ditch. It was there he lost his reputation. When he faced the first flume, spanning a hair-raising gorge, narrow, without railings, with a bellowing waterfall above, another below, and directly beneath a wild cascade, the air filled with driving spray and rocking to the clamor and rush of sound and motion—well, that cowboy dismounted from his horse, explained briefly that he had a wife and two children, and crossed over on foot, leading the horse behind him.

The only relief from the flumes was the precipices; and the only relief from the precipices was the flumes, except where the ditch was far underground, in which case we crossed one horse and rider at a time, on primitive log bridges that swayed and teetered and threatened to carry away. I confess that at first I rode such places with my feet loose in the stirrups, and that on the sheer walls I saw to it, by a definite, conscious act of will, that the foot in the outside stirrup, overhanging the thousand feet of fall, was exceedingly loose. I say "at first"; for, as in the crater itself we quickly lost our conception of magnitude, so, on the Nahiku Ditch, we quickly lost our apprehension of depth. The ceaseless iteration of height and depth produced a state of consciousness in which height and depth were accepted as the ordinary conditions of existence; and from the horse's back to look sheer down four hundred or five hundred feet became quite commonplace and nonproductive of thrills. And as carelessly as the trail and the horses, we swung along the dizzy heights and ducked around or through the waterfalls.

And such a ride! Falling water was everywhere. We rode above the clouds, under the clouds, and through the clouds! and every now and then a shaft of sunshine penetrated like a searchlight to the depths yawning beneath us, or flashed upon some pinnacle of the crater rim thousands of feet above. At every turn of the trail a waterfall or a dozen waterfalls, leaping hundreds of feet through the air, burst upon our vision. At our first night's camp, in the Keanae Gulch, we counted thirty-two waterfalls from a single viewpoint. The vegetation ran riot over that wild land. There were forests of koa and kolea trees, and candlenut trees; and then there were the trees called ohia-ai, which bore red mountain apples, mellow and juicy and most excellent to eat. Wild bananas grew everywhere, clinging to the sides of the gorges, and, overborne by their great bunches of ripe fruit, falling across the trail and blocking the way. And over the forest surged a sea of green life, the climbers of a thousand varieties, some that floated airily, in lacelike filaments, from the tallest branches; others that coiled and wound about the trees like huge serpents; and one, the ie-ie, that was for all the world like a climbing palm, swinging on a thick stem from branch to branch and tree to tree and throttling the supports whereby it climbed. Through the sea of green, lofty tree ferns thrust their great delicate fronds, and the lehua flaunted its scarlet blossoms. Underneath the climbers, in no less profusion, grew the warm-colored, strangely marked plants that in the United States one is accustomed to seeing preciously conserved in hothouses. In fact, the ditch country of Maui is nothing more nor less than a huge conservatory. Every familiar variety of fern flourishes, and more varieties that are unfamiliar, from the tiniest maidenhair to the gross and voracious staghorn, the latter the terror of the woodsmen, interlacing with itself in tangled masses five or six feet deep and covering acres.

Never was there such a ride. For two days it lasted, when we emerged into rolling country, and, along an actual wagon road, came home to the ranch at a gallop. I know it was cruel to gallop the horses after such a long, hard journey; but we blistered our hands in vain effort to hold them in. That's the sort of horses they grow on Haleakala. At the ranch there was a great festival of cattle driving, branding, and horse breaking. Overhead Ukiukiu and Naulu battled valiantly, and far above, in the sunshine, towered the mighty summit of Haleakala.

Heavenly Hana

Heavenly Hana! Greener than Eden!
Watered and warmed by our God above!
What shall we grow here?
What shall we show here?
The trees of Truth, Faith, Hope and Love*

by Richard J. Pietschmann

A resident of Los Angeles, Richard J. Pietschmann has written articles for Travel and Leisure, Bon Appetit, *and other publications. He is a contributing editor for* Los Angeles *magazine.*

Hymns sung in Hawaiian filter from two nearby churches through fragrant butter-yellow and magenta plumeria blossoms. I slump in the slanting morning sunlight on my lanai at the Hotel Hana-Maui, dissipating my morning torpor with a cup of Kona's finest, made moments ago in my plantation-posh room. Silent thanks are offered to the management for supplying whole coffee beans, a machine to grind them and another to brew them. Such welcome surprises in such a removed, ethereal place.

It is odd but fascinating to hear familiar hymns transmuted into Polynesian dialect, and I actually heave myself up in curiosity and stumble with cup in hand across the hotel's broad central lawn to squint through an archway at the 150-year-old Wananalua Congregational Church. The singing swells dramatically through the old church's open doors and then fades into the rustle of palm fronds and the faint slapping of swells against a rocky shoreline. Not even the shrill cry of an annoyed mynah can break the reflective spell.

As the hymn ends I head back to my lanai, mostly awake but lost in the kind of dreamy contemplation that Hana often induces. I had read that the church's walls, 2½ feet thick at the base, were constructed in 1842 by local volunteers directed by a Yankee *kahu* (shepherd or pastor), the Rev. Daniel Conde. The walls were built of volcanic stone, much of it scavenged from the ruins of the many ancient and highly sacred *heiaus* (shrines or temples) dotting this once heavily populated coastline. The mortar was made from coral brought up from depths of two or three fathoms by pure-blooded Hawaiians diving from ancestral canoes.

The church, like everything else along this storied eastern coast, is interwoven with the legends, history and people of the remote, rainy area. The way things interconnect here is frequently so eerie that the strains of the *Twilight Zone* theme begin playing unbidden in the back of your mind. A heightened sense of the physical and the spiritual binds the inhabitants of this extraordinary place into a dedicated community of protectors of its legend, superstition and beauty.

---

*second verse of the "Hanna Hymn," as translated from the Hawaiian

Even the Hotel Hana-Maui, first opened in 1946 (and ever since the sophisticated centerpiece of this otherwise rural area) is inexorably intertwined with the community. Along with the surrounding 4,500-acre Hana Ranch, it was rescued from decrepitude in 1984 by Texas oil heiress Caroline Rose Hunt's Rosewood Corporation. It is certainly one of the most casually luxurious—and expensive—hotels in Hawaii.

The small hotel alone received a $24 million renovation in 1987 that added rooms, rebuilt most others, completely remodeled the lobby, library, dining room and bar. What had been a slowly moldering pile was transformed into a showcase of tasteful design, quiet luxury and innovative menus thoroughly unexpected in such a bucolic environment. Spaces that before were dim and enclosed are now open and airy. Granite flagstones, bleached wood, skylights and masses of cut flowers add to the air of costly ease.

Newer guests have been surprised that the hotel is set in the midst of the modest town of Hana rather than plunked on some pristine beach, as its cachet and price might suggest. Traffic from the one main road chugs by just feet from many of the rooms, and the most expensive accommodations in the new Sea Ranch Cottages are a considerable stroll away, across another well-used public road. The community tennis courts and ball field lie adjacent, a lob away between Hana Bay and the hotel. This is no remote hideaway, at least not in the Robinson Crusoe sense.

Visitors to Hana have little choice, for example, but to join the estimated 1,500 sightseers who come daily in rental cars or on van tours to rubberneck through town, pause for lunch, lurch out to see the Seven Pools of Oheo Gulch, perhaps search futilely for Lindbergh's grave in Kipahulu and then turn around for the long drive back. If they want to stay overnight, alternatives to the Hotel Hana-Maui are the decidedly funky little Heavenly Hana Inn, the nice but few condo units of the Hana Kai-Maui Resort, or one of the private houses that can be booked through Hana Bay Vacation Rentals. Added together, there are only about 100 rooms for rent at Hana.

It rains a lot here: in the average year, 70 to 100 inches, and more than that just up the slope of two-mile-high Haleakala, whose largely unseen bulk looms over the rugged coastline its eruptions created. All of Hawaii's islands have a wet and a dry side, created by the convergence of steady trade winds and high mountains. On Maui, resort areas like Kaanapali Beach are on the arid leeward coasts, which have better beaches and a reliably sunny climate. Not so with lush, green Hana. The rain comes year-round, though much of it falls at night and in the early morning, and the most popular months of December and January, along with November, February and March, are the rainiest of all. Then it comes at any time and in frequent downpours, causing visitors to seek indoor entertainment that largely does not exist here. Scenic drives, beach barbecues, horseback rides, hiking, jogging, bicycling and the other normally wonderful outdoor diversions popular at Hana do not tend to be successful in wet weather. And the limited under-cover activities, such as a visit to the Hana Cultural Center, seem to use up minutes instead of hours. The Hotel Hana-Maui has a well-stocked library but no television or radio in the rooms.

But, of course, unending activity and utter comfort are not the things that have made Hana so alluring for so long to so many different people. Ex-Beatle George Harrison, Jim Nabors and other celebrities chose to live part-time in the Hana area because of the seclusion and the deep sense of physical and spiritual wonder. At Henry Kahula's Chevron station the windows are signed in grease pencil by entertainers like Kris Kristofferson and Steve Forrest.

The real Hana takes a while to work its peculiar magic on visitors. It is in the air all around, in this place where cultures gracefully glance off one another and legends mix as freely with facts as the broad-faced Hawaiians intermingle with the town's anachronistic contingent of backwoods hippies. One moment you will see two Hawaiians peacefully lounging in a pickup truck parked at the end of the old sugarcane-loading wharf that juts into Hana Bay quietly smoking *pakalolo* (marijuana), and the next, there is a placid blond, barefoot haole padding happily along Hana Highway as calves packed against a fence moo and eye her curiously. It is the sort of place where the Bank of Hawaii—the only bank—opens for 1½ hours every weekday except Friday (clearly the big day of the week), when it's open for three hours.

Sitting in the hotel's airy dining room eating banana waffles with ginger syrup—a breakfast as trendily correct as it is jarring and unlikely in such a determinedly retro place—my gaze rises from the torch ginger in the gardens to the modest mound of Kauiki Hill standing at one arm of Hana Bay. Clouds brush over the low ironwood-covered cinder cone, stirring up stories from the past.

In legend, it was here that the lovers Kauiki and Noenoe were forever united by the demigod Maui, who changed them into a hill and the mist that clings to it. In reality, it was the birthplace in 1768 of Queen Kaahumanu, Kamehameha the Great's favorite wife and later the regent, who turned Hawaii away from the past by fostering the breaking of the old kapus (taboos) and converting to Christianity. And it was around this ancient natural fortress that bloody battles raged for control of the coveted region.

Hana has always been cherished and important. Before the arrival of the first European ships offshore in the mid-1700s, Hana's rich agricultural lowland and forested upper reaches supported an estimated 45,000 to 75,000 people. The population had dropped to about 11,000 by 1831, and despite the importation of contract labor from China, Japan and other countries during the sugarcane boom that started in 1864, it's dwindled steadily ever since. In the 1930s, when the plantations began to close and various agricultural experiments failed, people began leaving at an even greater rate. A stabilized population of about a thousand people occupies the district today, many of predominantly Hawaiian blood, others bliss-seeking haole or the descendants of Chinese, Japanese and Portuguese workers.

In Hana, the issues of growth and tourism are as hotly debated and uses of the land are as fiercely contested as when armies fought over it in past centuries. Isolation and attitude discourages development and, sometimes, even curiosity here. Residents are fiercely protective of the land, chary of change. They will not hear of plans to expand the tiny airport so it can accommodate jets.

In this place of almost-mesmerizing tranquillity, the most peaceful, serene spot touched by man must be Palapala Hoomau Congregational Church, a place I find purely by instinct and have visited four times without encountering another human being. You drive out past Hana about 10 miles on a road far worse and more tortuous than the serpentine highway to the town, past the place called Seven Pools that is the terminus of most day tours, past the scattered ramshackle and grand houses of Kipahulu, past tiny St. Paul's Church and, on the right, the nearly hidden massive chimney of a ruined sugar mill.

Just past the mill, on the left side of the road, is a pasture and then a galvanized-steel gate swung permanently open on a rutted track that heads toward the sea. The road goes to the Palapala Hoomau Congregational Church, a few hundred yards away, mostly hidden behind thick vegetation. There is no sign on the road and nothing at all to indicate that anything lies down this country lane, but unlike the other gates in the area this one has no "kapu" or "keep out" sign. Founded in 1857 and built in 1864, the simple one-room church sits on a bluff over the sea, with a small graveyard on the ocean side.

It is a place of such healing aura and calming silence that the temptation is overwhelming to linger, to sit in the quiet, musty church reading the program from the last service—the call to worship, doxology and three hymns in Hawaiian—and then to stroll around the grounds. It is small wonder that Charles A. Lindbergh loved it so that he wanted his grave here. There it is, dated 1974, with three tiny American flags planted in the soil. Almost no one ever finds it.

At dusk on the way back to Hana, just after passing a grinning Hawaiian with his handsome small son, and driving cautiously along the bad road, I glanced up to see a small snow-white owl perched on a wire, gazing down at me. It was a *pueokea*, the rarely seen and endangered Hawaiian owl, a sighting some locals later told me was fraught with good fortune, for it is a blessing promising a safe journey. Minutes later I saw a second, also curiously watching me. This, I was told, was almost unprecedented. I was regarded with new respect in Hana. I might be home.

Highway to Hana

*by Richard J.
Pietschmann*

The road to Hana is paved, I was told, with rude inventions. For starters, its 44 spine-tingling miles were said to contain 56 one-lane bridges—guaranteed to elevate adrenaline to levels associated with such activities as gladiatorial combat—along with precisely 617 whirligig curves, several stretches of one-way traffic, innumerable potholes, much evidence of recent washouts, a few crumbled cliffsides and significant numbers of pinprick-pupiled tourists whose fingers would have to be removed surgically from the steering wheels of their rental cars.

This run of fabled highway along Maui's wild, windward, sparsely populated and stunningly scenic northeast coast seemed to have been the scene of countless cases of cracked nerves and hair-raising mishaps, dreadful weather and backed-up traffic. "I just *hate* that drive," said the waitress at Mama's Fish House outside Paia (usually cited as the beginning point for the journey) as she cleaned up the remains of my *ahi* sandwich just before I hit the road. "Something *always* happens."

I knew better. During three previous trips on the Hana Highway nothing particularly untoward had occurred, except a bit of hesitant traffic and some light rain, along with plenty of gorgeous scenery. And travel time was well below the 2½-hour minimum quoted to timid tourists. On the last run, in fact, I had established a personal best of less than 1½ hours from Hana to Paia—in an open Jeep, to boot. Sure, occasional mists descended to dampen my baseball cap, tires sometimes squealed around some of the more serious switchbacks, and a backseat passenger emerged at the end dazed and hobbling but grinning happily.

The mostly two-lane road—ancient footpaths widened by convict gangs in 1926, paved in 1962 and upgraded into passable shape for normal traffic only in 1982—is in fairly good shape. But all that weather and those winter washouts tend to age the road quickly in its more vulnerable spots, so don't expect smooth sailing for the entire length. The two slowest stretches have many places where 10 mph is the norm, and careful drivers inch around the hairpins much more slowly than that.

But what a small price to pay for such a spectacular journey—through rain forest and jungle, past streams and waterfalls, with postcard vistas of windswept peninsulas, deep bays and green valleys. Tiny villages, each centered by a steepled church, pop up unexpectedly in the midst of all this natural grandeur. The sprinkling of people, most with a high percentage of Polynesian blood, live simply, farming taro, bananas and other crops. It's not hard to see why this part of Maui is called the true Hawaii, away from any sign of tourism or commerce.

Easily distracted from missions of most sorts, I made it only a couple of miles past Mama's to Hookipa Beach Park, situated on a windy bluff overlooking the most famous wind-surfing waters in the world. Usually, one quick look at the scores of boards with brightly colored sails skipping through and flipping over the churning waves is fortifying enough to make the most harrowing drive seem dull and uneventful. Not today, though. It was so rough and windy that even the notoriously devil-may-care wind surfers had furled their sails and slunk back to the saloons of Paia. No matter. Hana, ho.

The drive was actually fun as well as beautiful, and the one-way bridges over steep gullies were welcome opportunities to slow and even pause to gaze at the rain forest and stream-fed waterfalls. The wonder of Hawaii's renowned microclimates becomes gradually evident as the drive unfolds from rolling pastureland to jungled cliffs sliced by narrow valleys, and then level tropical upland.

The modest tongue of flat land that is the Keanae Peninsula materializes suddenly, its simple weathered church and taro patches a shock after miles of rain forest. Just beyond, spread far below the road, is the community of Wailua, its white steepled church boldly visible from the great distance. Then the jungle closes in to swallow a road that once more plunges in cramped surrender.

During previous drives I had been fascinated by a tree whose spade-shaped leaves shimmered so filmily from above that the jungle below appeared like a sea of glistening white. I stopped to follow a stream a short distance until I found one of those trees and picked a leaf. A gardener at the Hotel Hana-Maui later identified it as from the Kukui tree—one of the few native trees able to compete with such imported varieties as guava, mango, eucalyptus and bamboo that now dominate the forest. Even the wild white and torch ginger that bloom along the roadside are imports.

Toward the end, just a few miles outside Hana and giddy with the pleasant vertigo of it all, I began drifting into some other road-warrior dimension. Here as the highway begins to untwist, drivers are lulled into thinking they can relax, but another series of one-lane bridges appears. By then I was making up stories for each bridge, at one noting mynah birds standing guard "like tiny Horatios." Ninety minutes after stopping at Hookipa to look for windsurfers, the drive was over.

I thought that was *hauling* until Clyde Min, who manages the Hotel Hana-Maui, casually mentioned that his best-ever time was at night after dinner at Mama's. No traffic. No sightseeing. And all in 50 minutes flat. He swears.

3 Exploring Maui

A visitor to Maui has plenty of things to see and do besides spending time on the beach. To help you organize your time, this guide divides the island into four tours—West Maui, Central Maui, Haleakala and Upcountry, and the Road to Hana (East Maui). Each tour lasts from a half day to a full day, depending on how long you spend at each stop. All tours require a car, but they include opportunities for walking.

In getting yourself oriented, first look at a map of Maui. You will notice two distinct circular land masses, each volcanic in origin, which means that mountains dominate both centers. The smaller lump of land, on the western part of the island, is home to the 5,788-foot Puu Kukui range, some of its reaches now used to grow sugar and pineapple. Occasionally, hardy souls try to hike the Puu Kukui mountains, but there aren't marked trails, and the views aren't that spectacular. Along the western shore of this land mass is the area known as West Maui, where most of the island's visitor industry has established itself. West Maui is sunny and warm year-round.

The larger land mass of the eastern portion of Maui was created by Haleakala, the mist-covered peak in the center. One of the best-known mountains in the Pacific, Haleakala is popular for hiking and sightseeing. This larger region of the island is called East Maui, with the areas of Wailea, Kihei, and Makena flanking its western shore, while Hana and its wilder environs— past where the pavement stops—sit on the eastern seaboard.

Between the two mountain areas is Central Maui, which was once the ocean until Haleakala spewed lava into the channel separating East from West. Central Maui is the location of the county seat of Wailuku, from which the islands of Maui, Lanai, Molokai, and Kahoolawe are governed. Most of the island's commerce and industry is based in Central Maui; a majority of Maui's businesspeople work in Kahului and Wailuku.

Highlights for First-time Visitors

Alexander & Baldwin Sugar Museum, Tour 2
Baldwin Home, Tour 1
Brig *Carthaginian II*, Tour 1
Hale Hoikeike, Tour 2
Haleakala, Tour 3
Hana, Tour 4
Helani Gardens, Tour 4
Hookipa Beach, Tour 4
Iao Valley, Tour 4
Lahaina, Tour 1
Paia, Tour 4
Tedeschi Vineyards and Winery, Tour 3

Tour 1: West Maui

Numbers in the margin correspond with points of interest on the Exploring Maui map.

Drive about as far north as you can on the Honoapiilani Highway (Highway 30), and make a left on Bay Drive at the Kapalua sign. We'll start this tour at the **Kapalua Bay Hotel** (1 Bay Dr., tel. 808/669–5656), set in a beautifully secluded location in upper West Maui. Surrounded by pineapple fields, this classy hotel was built in 1978 by Maui Land & Pineapple Company and now hosts celebrities who want to be left alone, as well as some of the world's richest folks. The Kapalua Villas are expansive condominiums on the resort property that start at $275 a night. Kapalua's shops and restaurants are some of Maui's finest, but expect to pay big bucks for whatever you purchase (*see* Chapters 4 and 6 for more details).

Back in the car, return from the hotel to Honoapiilani Highway and make a left. Drive north, and in less than a mile the road is less well maintained. This used to be the route to Wailuku. It was never a good road, and a storm a few years back made it partly impassable. That means you may eventually have to turn back before reaching Wailuku. However, you'll discover some gorgeous photo opportunities along the road, and if you go far ❷ enough, you'll come to **Kahakuloa,** a tiny fishing village that seems lost in time. It is one of the oldest towns on Maui. Many remote villages that were similar to Kahakuloa used to be tucked away in the valleys of this area. This is the wild side of West Maui; true adventurers will find terrific snorkeling and swimming here, as well as some good hiking trails.

Kahakuloa is about as far as you can go on the "highway" that alternates between being called 30 and 340. From Kahakuloa, turn around and go back in the direction from which you came—south toward Kaanapali and Lahaina. Along the way to Kaanapali, you'll pass the beach towns of **Napili, Kahana,** and **Honokowai,** which are packed with condos and a few restaurants. Some of this area can be charming; if you wish to explore these towns, get off the Upper Honoapiilani Highway and drive closer to the water.

Time Out If it's Monday or Thursday, check out the **Farmer's Market** in Kahana. County Council member Wayne Nishiki sets up his open-air fruit-and-veggie show in the parking lot at the ABC Store at 3511 Lower Honoapiilani Highway. The Farmer's Market specializes in quality produce at reasonable prices, and, of course, there's the flamboyant Nishiki himself. *Open Mon. 12:30–4:30, Thurs. 9–noon.*

❸ If you're staying at the **Kaanapali Beach Resort,** save exploring it for another day. Otherwise, you may want to see two hotels at Kaanapali, the **Hyatt Regency Maui** (200 Nohea Kai Dr., 808/661–1234) and the **Westin Maui** (2365 Kaanapali Pkwy., 808/667–2525). To reach these properties, from Kahakuloa take the third Kaanapali exit on Honoapiilani Highway (the one closest to Lahaina), then turn left on Kaanapali Parkway. Although the resort has six hotels and seven condos, the Hyatt and Westin hotels are of special interest because they were both built by Honolulu-based developer Christopher Hemmeter, whose resort projects have grown more and more opulent over the years. The Hyatt, for example, was built in 1980 at a cost of about $80 million. It has a waterfall in the swimming pool and eight more falls scattered around the property. The Westin, a $155 million makeover of the much older Maui Surf Hotel, also has waterfalls all over the place—15 at last count. Its extensive art collection, worth about $2 million, includes work from around the world, with an emphasis on Asian and Pacific art.

Kaanapali Beach Resort also has some decent shopping at the **Whalers Village** (2435 Kaanapali Pkwy., tel. 808/661–4567), with such trendy mainland shops as ACA Joe, Benetton, and

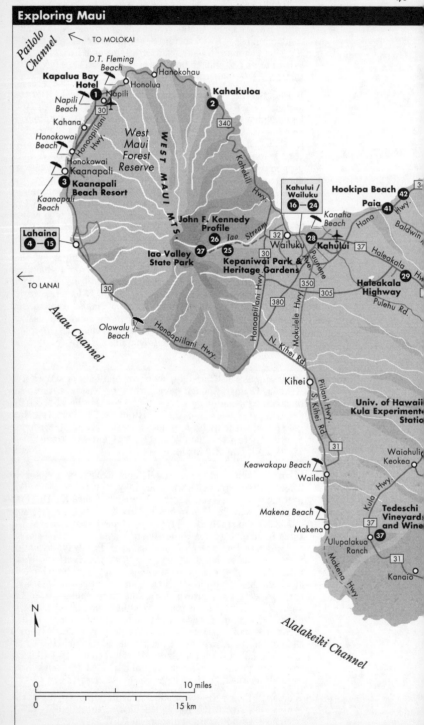

Pailolo Channel

← TO MOLOKAI

D.T. Fleming Beach

Kapalua Bay Hotel
①

Honokohau

Kahakuloa
②

Honolua

Napili Beach
Napili

30

Kahana

Honokowai Beach

Honokowai

Kaanapali

340

West Maui Forest Reserve

③ Kaanapali Beach Resort

Kaanapali Beach

W E S T   M A U I   M T S.

Kahekili Hwy.

Kahului / Wailuku
⑯ — ㉔

Hookipa Beach **㊷**
Paia **㊶**

3

Kanaha Beach

Lahaina
④ — ⑮

John F. Kennedy Profile
㉖

Iao Stream

㉘
Kahului

Hana Hwy.

Baldwin

㉗
Iao Valley State Park

㉕

Wailuku

32

37

Haleakala Hwy.

Kepaniwai Park & Heritage Gardens

30

Puunene Ave.

← TO LANAI

Anau Channel

350

305

Haleakala Highway

㉙

Olowalu Beach

Honoapiilani Hwy.

Honoapiilani Hwy.

380

Mokulele Hwy.

Pulehu Rd.

N. Kihei Rd.

Kihei

Piilani Hwy.

S. Kihei Rd.

Univ. of Hawaii Kula Experiment Station

31

Waiohuli
Keokea

Keawakapu Beach

Wailea

Kula Hwy.

Makena Beach

Tedeschi Vineyard and Wine

Makena

37
㊲

Ulupalakua Ranch

31

Makena Hwy.

Kanaio

N
↑

Alalakeiki Channel

0		10 miles
0		15 km

PACIFIC OCEAN

Ulumalu Rd.

365

Huelo 43

Kailua
360

390

Kokomo

Puohokamoa
Stream 44 45 Kaumahina State
Wayside Park

10 Makawao

Honomanu 46
Valley 47 Keanae Arboretum

Pukalani

377

Keanae Overlook 48 Wailua
49 Wailua Lookout

50 51 Nahiku

Waikane
Falls

Pitman Stream

Haleakala
Crater Rd.

Koolau
Forest
Reserve

360 Hana Hwy.

Waianapanapa
State Park

52

Park
Headquarters/
Visitor Center

7

Leleiwi
Overlook 30

378 31

Helani Gardens 53
Hotel Hana-Maui 55 Hana
54

Hana Forest Reserve

38

36 Kula Botanical
Gardens

32

Kalahaku
Overlook

Haleakala
National Park

Haleamuu Trail

Hamoa

Mt. Haleakala 35 33

Puu Ulaula 34 Haleakala Visitor
Overlook Center

Kaupo Trail

Piilani Hwy.

Muolea

Kahikinui
Forest Reserve

56 Oheo Gulch

Kipahulu

31

57 Grave of
Charles Lindbergh

Piilani Hwy.

Kaupo

31

Alenuihaha Channel

TO HAWAII ↓

Esprit, as well as such Hawaiian boutiques as Blue Ginger Designs, Paradise Clothing, and Lahaina Printsellers.

❹ Back in the car, it's time to head for **Lahaina.** This little whaling town has a notorious past; there are stories of lusty whalers who met head-on with missionaries bent on saving souls. Both groups journeyed to Lahaina from New England in the early 1800s. To get oriented, take a drive down **Front Street.** At first, Lahaina might look touristy, but there's a lot that's genuine here as well. Lahaina has recently been concentrating on the renovation of its old buildings, which date from the time it was Hawaii's capital, in the 1800s. Much of the town has been designated a National Historic Landmark; further restrictions have been imposed on all new buildings, which must resemble structures built before 1920.

Numbers in the margin correspond with points of interest on the Lahaina map.

❺ One result of this reconstruction is **505 Front Street** at the southern end of Front Street, where you can park. Quaint New England–style architecture characterizes this mall, which houses small shops connected by a wooden sidewalk. It isn't as crowded as some other areas in Lahaina, probably because between here and the nearby Banyan Tree, the town turns into a sleepy residential neighborhood and some people give up before reaching the mall. A local hangout called **Sam's Pub,** however, seems to lure its fair share of fun-lovers.

❻ The **Banyan Tree,** which is a short walk from 505 Front Street, was planted in 1873. It is the largest of its kind in the 50th state and provides a welcome retreat for the weary who come to sit under its awesome branches. When the sun sets each evening, mynah birds settle in for a screeching symphony (which can be ❼ an event in itself). Next to the tree is the **Court House,** which now houses two art galleries—one upstairs and one in what was an old prison in the basement. The Court House was originally built in 1859 and rebuilt in 1925. *649 Wharf St., tel. 808/ 661–0111. Admission free. Open daily 10–4.*

❽ About a half block northwest, you'll find what's left of a **Brick Palace** built by King Kamehameha I, as well as the four cannons he used to protect it. Actually, nothing much remains of the palace, so don't waste time looking for a building. All that's left is a space with several holes sectioned off in front of the Pioneer Inn, one of Hawaii's oldest hotels. Hawaii's first king lived only one year in the palace because his favorite wife, Kaahumanu, refused to stay there. After 70 years, it collapsed.

❾ The **Brig *Carthaginian II*** is anchored at the dock nearby and is open as a museum. It was made in Germany in the 1920s and is a replica of the type of ship that brought the missionaries around the Horn to Hawaii in the early 1800s. The Brig *Carthaginian II* is the only authentically restored square-rigged brig in the world. A small museum below deck features a film and exhibit about whaling. *At the harbor, tel. 808/661–3262. Admission: $3. Open daily 9–4:30.*

Time Out If you're in the mood for some local color, stroll into the **Pioneer** ❿ **Inn** (658 Wharf St., tel. 808/661–3636) for a refreshment. This hotel, built in 1920, has a few inexpensive rooms upstairs and a restaurant. The inn's ambience capitalizes on Lahaina's whaling era, during the 19th century. This is where the cruise-boat

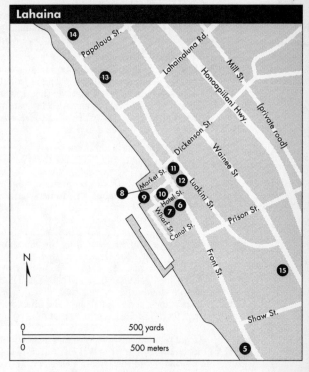

captains, fishermen, and brave tourists hang out during the afternoon. It can be fun or a little freaky, depending on how much everyone's had to drink and on your point of view.

If you walk from the *Carthaginian II* to the corner of Front and Dickenson streets, you'll find the **Baldwin Home.** An early missionary to Lahaina, Ephraim Spaulding, built this plastered and whitewashed coral stone home in 1834–35; in 1836 Dr. Dwight Baldwin—also a missionary—moved in with his family. The home is now run by the Lahaina Restoration Foundation and has been restored and furnished in a decor that reflects the period. You can view the living room with the family's grand piano, the dining room, the master bedroom with Dr. and Mrs. Baldwin's four-poster koa wood bed, and the boys' bedroom. Dr. Baldwin's dispensary is also on display, including his Hawaiian medical license. *696 Front St., tel. 808/661–3262. Admission: $2. Open daily 9–4:30.*

Next door is the **Master's Reading Room,** Maui's oldest building, constructed in 1833. In the early days, the ground floor was a mission's storeroom, while the reading room upstairs was for sailors. The **Lahaina Restoration Foundation** is housed in the building.

Continue north or south on **Front Street** for Lahaina's commercial side. Shops abound here; some are funky, a few are exquisite. Several little malls go back off the street, and some of the unique stores can be found there. Lahaina also boasts so many fine art galleries that it's occasionally referred to as SoHo West (*see* Shopping, below). At the Wharf Cinema Center (658 Front

⑫ St.), you can see the **Spring House,** which was built by missionaries over a freshwater spring. The building is now home to a
huge Fresnel lens once used in a local lighthouse that guided
ships to Lahaina.

⑬ If you continue north on Front Street, you'll pass the **Wo Hing
Society,** originally built as a temple in 1912. It now contains
Chinese artifacts and a historic theater that features Thomas
Edison films of Hawaii, circa 1898. Upstairs is the only public
Taoist altar on Maui. *858 Front St., tel. 808/661–3262. Admis-
sion free. Open daily 9–4:30.*

⑭ Head another block north and you'll find the **Seamen's Hospital,**
which was built in the 1830s as a royal party house for King Kamehameha III. It was later turned over to the U.S. government, which used it as a hospital for whaling men. Now within
the building, **Lahaina Printsellers** sells antique maps and
charts. *1024 Front St., tel. 808/661–3262. Admission free.
Open daily.*

Time Out There's nothing like watching the sun sink in the western sky
while you sit near the ocean. In Lahaina, a couple of restaurants have situated their lanais right over the water. Try
Kimo's (845 Front St., tel. 808/661–4811). Here, you can have
simple food and a relaxing drink while you watch the
parasailors, the cruise boats, and other water fanatics work in
the last minutes of another great day.

If you're finished walking before dusk with a hankering for just
⑮ one more stop, try the **Waiola Church** (535 Wainee St., tel. 808/
661–4349) and the **Waiola Cemetery.** To reach the church and
cemetery, walk south down Front Street, make a left onto
Dickenson Street, then make a right onto Wainee Street and
walk another few blocks. The cemetery is the older of the two
sites, dating from the time when Kamehameha's sacred wife
Queen Keopuolani died and was buried there in 1823. The
church was erected next door in 1832 by Hawaiian chiefs and
was originally named Ebenezer by the queen's second husband, Governor Hoapili. It was later named Wainee, after the
district in which it is located. After a few fires and some wind
damage, the current structure was put up in 1953 and named
Waiola Church.

Tour 2: Central Maui

*Numbers in the margin correspond with points of interest on
the Kahului–Wailuku map.*

This tour begins in **Kahului,** which looks nothing like the lush
tropical paradise most people envision when they think of Hawaii. This industrial and commercial town is home to many of
Maui's permanent residents, who find their jobs and the center
of commerce close by. Kahului was built in the early 1950s as
the answer to Alexander & Baldwin's problems. This large
company was tired of playing landlord to its many plantation
workers and sold land to a developer who promised to create af-
fordable housing. The scheme worked, and Kahului became the
first planned city in Hawaii. Most tourists spend little time
here, merely passing through on their way to and from the airport. Kaahumanu Avenue (Hwy. 32) is Kahului's main street
and runs east and west.

Kahului does have Maui's largest shopping mall, the
(16) **Kaahumanu Center** (275 Kaahumanu Ave., tel. 808/877–3369).
You might want to stop in at **Camellia Seed Shop** for what the
locals call "crack seed," a delicacy that's made from dried
fruits, nuts, and sugar. Other places to shop at Kaahumanu
Center include **Shirokiya,** a major department store brought to
Hawaii from Japan, and such American standards as Mrs.
Field's Cookies, Sears, Kay-Bee Toys, and Kinney Shoes.

(17) Next take a detour to visit the **Alexander & Baldwin Sugar Museum.** Get on Kaahumanu Avenue from the shopping center
and take a right onto Highway 350 (Puunene Ave.). Look for
the museum just off Highway 350 as you drive into the town
called Puunene (pronounced *Poo-nay-NAY*) in the direction of
Wailea. You'll be heading toward **Haleakala,** a 10,023-foot dormant volcano, which you should save most of a day to explore
(*see* Tour 3, below). Alexander & Baldwin, Maui's largest land-
owner, opened this museum in 1988 to detail the rise of sugarcane in the Islands. Alexander & Baldwin was one of five companies, better known as the Big Five, that spearheaded the
planting, harvesting, and marketing of the valuable agricultural product. Although Hawaiian sugar has been supplanted by
cheaper foreign versions—as well as by less costly sugar
beets—for many years, the crop was the mainstay of the Hawaiian economy.

The museum is located in a small, restored plantation-mana-
ger's house next to the post office and the still-operating sugar
mill. At the refinery, black smoke billows up when cane is burn-
ing; from the outside, the whole operation looks dirty and industrial. Inside the museum, you'll find historic photos, artifacts, and documents that explain the introduction of
sugarcane to Hawaii and how plantation managers brought in
laborers from other countries, thereby changing the Islands'
ethnic mix. This fascinating exhibit is well worth your time.
*3957 Hansen Rd., Puunene, tel. 808/871–8058. Admission: $2
adults, $1 students 6–17. Open Mon.–Sat. 9:30–4:30.*

Time Out As you return to Kahului, head toward the Kaahumanu Center.
When you reach the corner of Puunene and Kaahumanu
(18) avenues, you'll be at the **Kahului Shopping Center.** Here you'll
find **Ah Fook's Super Market** (tel. 808/877–3308), a local-style
grocery where you can also get genuine Japanese, Chinese, and
Hawaiian food. There are no tables, but the shady mall offers a
quiet stopping spot.

Return to Kaahumanu Avenue, head toward Wailuku, and take
a right onto Kahului Beach Road. Here you can see any ships in
(19) port at **Kahului Harbor.** This is Maui's chief port, since it's the
island's only deep-draft harbor. Cruise ships call here, as do
large freighters and tugboats. Surfers sometimes use this spot
as a castoff to catch some good waves, but it's not a good swimming beach.

Continue on the beach road until you reach Kanaloa Avenue,
(20) make a left and soon you'll find **Maui Zoological and Botanical
Gardens.** This is a great spot for kids, since there's a small
children's zoo that includes peacocks, African pygmy goats,
spider monkeys, and lots more. The gardens of native Hawaiian
plants actually take a much smaller role in this attraction than

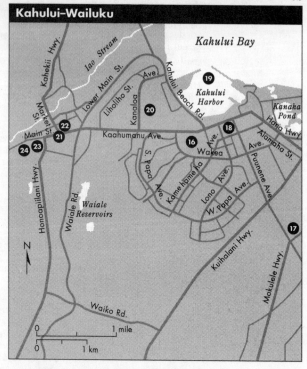

the name implies. *Kanaloa Ave. off Kaahumanu Ave., tel. 808/243–7337. Admission free. Open daily 9–4.*

Press on to Wailuku by turning right from Kanaloa Avenue back onto Kaahumanu Avenue. (Kaahumanu eventually becomes Wailuku's Main Street.) You'll soon reach **Wailuku's Historical District,** mostly concentrated on High Street, as well as around Vineyard and Market streets. Much of the area is in the Register of Historic Places, and many of the old buildings are being preserved with their wooden facades intact. Overall, the little town is sleepy and belies its function as Maui's county seat. Wailuku is where you'll see the County Court House (on the corner of Main St. and Honoapiilani Hwy.), from which Maui's first woman mayor, Linda Lingle, runs the county that includes the islands of Maui, Molokai, Lanai, and Kahoolawe.

In ancient times, Wailuku was a favored place for the inhabitants of Maui, who maintained two *heiaus* (temples) on the hills above. They used these heiaus primarily to watch for intruders, and villages grew up around the temples to support the cause. But the town really began to grow when the first missionaries arrived in the 1820s.

To get a closer look at this historical area, turn right at Market Street from Main Street, where you'll see the **Iao Theater** (68 N. Market St., tel. 808/242–6969), one of Wailuku's most photographed landmarks. This charming movie house went up in Wailuku in 1927 and acted as a community gathering spot. A few years ago, several ambitious developers almost had the community convinced that the theater should be gutted and re-

placed with brand-new shops and offices. But then the Maui
Community Theatre started using it as its headquarters. The
art deco–style building is now the focus of the Wailuku Main
Street Program. Unless there's a play on, you can't usually get
inside the theater.

Time Out   Stop off at **Hazel's** (2080 Vineyard, tel. 808/244–7278). Owner
Hazel Yasutomi serves no-nonsense food here—specialties
such as Spam and eggs, pork chops, and burgers. This is where
the locals hang out to enjoy the relaxed environment. You'll see
the Wailuku Grand Hotel nearby.

㉓ Next visit **Kaahumanu Church** (tel. 808/244–5189), which is on
High Street around the corner from Main Street and across the
way from the County Court House. It's said that Queen
Kaahumanu attended services on this site in 1832 and request-
ed that a permanent structure be erected. Builders first tried
adobe, which dissolved in the rain, then stone. The present
wooden structure, built in 1876, is classic New England style,
with white exterior walls and striking green trim. You won't be
able to see the interior, however, unless you attend Sunday services. The church features a Hawaiian service—completely in
Hawaiian—each Sunday at 9 AM.

Return to Main Street and drive away from Kahului. After a
㉔ few blocks, on your left, you'll see **Hale Hoikeike** (House of Display). This structure was the home of Edward and Caroline
Bailey, two prominent missionaries who came to Wailuku to
run the first Hawaiian girls' school on the island, the Wailuku
Female Seminary; this school's function was mainly to train the
girls in the "feminine arts."

Hale Hokeike's construction between 1833 and 1850 was super-
vised by Edward Bailey himself. The Maui Historical Society
has opened a museum in the plastered stone house, with displays of a small artifacts collection from before and after the
missionaries' arrival, and Mr. Bailey's paintings of Wailuku.
Some rooms are decorated with missionary-period furniture.
The Hawaiian Room has exhibits on the making of tapa cloth, as
well as samples of pre–Captain Cook weaponry. Unfortunately, the girls' school is no longer standing. *2375A Main St., tel.
808/244–3326. Suggested optional donation: $2 adults, 50¢
children. Open Mon.–Sat. 10–4:30.*

*Numbers in the margin correspond with points of interest on
the Exploring Maui map.*

Back on Main Street, drive toward the mountains for this tour's
last destination, Iao Needle. If you go straight, Main Street
turns into Iao Valley Road. Before you're even out of town, the
air cools and the hilly terrain gets more lush. Soon you'll come
㉕ to **Kepaniwai Park and Heritage Gardens.** This county park is
now a memorial to Maui's melting pot, with ethnic displays dotting the landscape. There's an early Hawaiian shack, a New
England saltbox, a Portuguese villa with gardens, and dwell-
ings from other cultures, such as China, the Philippines, and
Portugal. This is a lovely spot to take a break or bring a picnic
lunch.

However, the peacefulness here belies the history of the area.
During his quest for domination, King Kamehameha I brought
his troops to the Valley Isle in 1790 and engaged in a particular-

ly bloody battle near Kepaniwai Park. He succeeded in his plan
to defeat Maui and thereby take over the entire group of islands, but the result was mass murder. Bodies blocked Iao
Stream, so that the village downstream was given the name
Wailuku, which means "bloody river."

26 As you drive toward the needle, you'll come to a landmark
called **John F. Kennedy Profile.** The Hawaiians, it seems, can
see something in every rock formation throughout the Islands.
But this one does uncannily resemble the profile of the late
president.

27 Iao Valley Road ends at **Iao Valley State Park.** When Mark
Twain saw this park, he dubbed it the Yosemite of the Pacific.
Here you'll find the erosion-formed gray and moss-green rock
called **Iao Needle,** a spire that rises 1,200 feet from the valley
floor. You can take one of several easy hikes from the parking
lot across Iao Stream and explore the jungle-like area. This
park offers a beautiful set of walks, where you can stop and con-
template by the edge of a stream or look at some of the native
plants and flowers. Mist occasionally rises if there's been a rain,
making the spot even more magical. *Admission free. No set
hours.*

Tour 3: Haleakala and Upcountry

*Numbers in the margin correspond with points of interest on
the Exploring Maui map.*

The fertile western slopes leading up to majestic **Mt. Haleakala**
are called Upcountry. This region is responsible for much of
Hawaii's produce. Lettuce, tomatoes, and sweet Maui onions
are some of the most popular crops grown here, but the area is
also a big flower producer. As you drive along you'll notice plenty of natural vegetation, as clumps of cacti mingle with purple
jacaranda, wild hibiscus, and towering eucalyptus trees. Car-
nations are the number one flower in the area, but the exotic-
looking protea are rapidly gaining in popularity.

Upcountry is also fertile ranch land, with such spreads as the
30,000-acre Ulupalakua, long famous for raising cattle, and the
20,000-acre Haleakala Ranch, which throws its well-attended
rodeo each July 4th. In addition, Tedeschi Vineyards and Winery dominates Hawaii's only wine-producing region, just a few
acres of Ulupalakua land.

28 Start this tour of Haleakala in **Kahului.** Before setting out, call
808/871–5054 for Haleakala's weather conditions. Extreme
gusty winds, heavy rain, and even snow in winter are not
uncommon—even if it is paradise as usual down at beach level.
Because of the high altitude, the mountaintop temperature is
often as much as 30 degrees cooler than in sea-level Maui. If you
didn't pack a warm jacket or can't borrow one, skip watching
the sunrise until the next trip and settle for a morning or mid-
day visit.

29 After you've checked out the weather conditions, drive on **Haleakala Highway,** or Highway 37, toward the big mountain of
Haleakala (House of the Sun) in the center of the island. On this
road, you'll travel from sea level to 10,023 feet in only 38
miles—a feat you won't be able to repeat on any other car route
in the world. It's not a quick drive, however; it'll take you about
two hours. We recommend that you start fairly early in the

morning, since the clouds move over the top of the mountain as soon as 11 AM.

Try to make the drive up Haleakala without stopping, since you'll want the best views possible. Watch the signs, because Haleakala Highway will diverge in two directions. If you go straight, the road becomes Kula Highway, which is still Highway 37. If you veer to the left, the road becomes Highway 377. You want this latter road. After about 6 miles, make a left onto Haleakala Crater Road. The switchbacks begin here. With the ascent, you'll notice the weather getting a bit chilly. As you 30 near the top, there's a **Park Headquarters/Visitor Center,** where you can stop and orient yourself to the volcano's origins and eruption history. Mt. Haleakala is the centerpiece of the 27,284-acre Haleakala National Park, which was dedicated in 1961 to preserving the area. At the gift shop, you can get maps, as well as some nice posters and other memorabilia. *At the 7,000-ft elevation on Haleakala Crater Rd., tel. 808/572–9306. Cost: $3 car fee, $1 per person for hikers, senior citizens free. Visitor Center open daily 7:30–4.*

Several lookout areas are located within the park itself. The first you'll come to as you continue your ascent on Haleakala 31 Crater Road is **Leleiwi Overlook,** at about 8,800 feet elevation. There's parking here and the beginning of the Haleamauu Trail, which leads into the volcano crater. If you happen to be at this point in the late afternoon, it's possible you'll experience a phenomenon called the Brocken Specter. Named after a similar occurrence in East Germany's Harz Mountains, the "specter" allows you to see yourself reflected on the clouds and circled by a rainbow. Don't wait all day for this, because it is not an everyday thing.

32 Next is **Kalahaku Overlook,** a particularly interesting stop at about the 9,000-foot level. The famous silversword plant grows here amid the desertlike surroundings; in fact, the flowering plant grows in only one other place in the park, along the Halemauu Trail, within the crater. The silversword looks like a member of the yucca family and produces a stalk some 3 to 8 feet tall with several hundred yellow and purple flower heads. At this lookout, the silversword is kept in an enclosure to protect it from nibbling wildlife.

33 Next you'll come to **Haleakala Visitor Center,** at about 9,800 feet. By now you're about 10 miles from park headquarters, but a ranger is on duty here as well. The center has exhibits inside and a trailhead that leads to White Hill, a small crater nearby. This is a short, easy walk that will give you an even better view of the volcano crater. Shortly after noon each day, the ranger gives an informative lecture on Haleakala geology. In the summer, a 90-minute walk with a ranger guide that goes partly down Sliding Sands Trail starts daily at 9. *Center open sunrise–3.*

34 Continue on to reach the highest point on Maui, the **Puu Ulaula Overlook.** Here you'll find a glass-enclosed lookout that boasts a 360-degree view from the 10,023-foot summit. People gather here for the best sunrise view, as the building's open 24 hours a day. Sunrise generally begins between 5:45 and 7, depending on the time of year. On a clear day, you can see the islands of Molokai, Lanai, Kahoolawe, and the Big Island. On a *really* clear day, you can even spot Oahu glimmering in the distance.

On a small hill above, you'll see **Science City**, a research and communications center that looks like it's straight out of an espionage thriller. You can't visit the center, unfortunately, since the University of Hawaii and the Department of Defense don't allow visitors. The university maintains an observatory, while the Defense Department tracks satellites.

35 Now head back down the way you came and see the lower nooks and crannies of **Mt. Haleakala.** When you reach Highway 377 again, make a right.

Time Out Within about a quarter mile on Highway 377, you'll see **Kula Lodge** (Haleakala Hwy., tel. 808/878–2517). The lodge is a popular post–Haleakala-sunrise spot; it offers a hearty breakfast of the best eggs Benedict you'll find this side of the Rockies. The views are spectacular since the lodge has windows all around, which allows you to see all the way to the ocean. The flower fields outside are an added benefit.

36 Backtrack and stay on Highway 377 and then go past the 378 intersection for about 2 more miles, where you'll come to **Kula Botanical Gardens** on your left. Specimens grow somewhat naturally here, and you'll see all kinds of flora that may be unfamiliar. There are koa trees, often made into finely turned bowls and handcrafted furniture, and kukui trees (ancient Hawaiians used the tree's nuts, which are filled with oil, for lighting). In addition, the gardens have the requisite protea, varieties of ginger, and stands of bamboo orchid. *RR 2, Box 288, Upper Kula Rd., tel. 808/878–1715. $3 adults, 50¢ children 6–12. Open daily 9–4.*

37 Continue on Highway 377 away from Kahului and you'll soon join Highway 377 again. In about 8 miles, you'll come to **Tedeschi Vineyards and Winery,** where you can sample Hawaii's only homegrown wines: a pleasant Maui Blush, the Maui Brut-Blanc de Noirs Hawaiian Champagne, and Tedeschi's annual Maui Nouveau. You can also get a tour of the winery and purchase whatever wines you like. The most unusual wine, Maui Blanc, is made from pineapple concentrate; the winery owners started their operation by buying juice from their neighbor, Maui Land & Pineapple Company.

The winery's tasting room is unusual because it once served as the jail for James Makee's Rose Ranch, where the old-time farmer grew sugarcane back in the 1860s. A large plantation house perches on the slope above, dominating the scenery. Tedeschi is definitely worth a visit. *Ulupalakua Ranch, Haleakala Hwy., tel. 808/878–6058. Admission free. Open daily 9–5.*

38 Now return the way you came and head toward Kahului on Highway 37. When you get to the Highway 37/377 fork, bear to the left to stay on Highway 37. You're now on Kula Highway, which eventually turns back into Haleakala Highway (this isn't as confusing as it sounds). Within about 2 miles, you'll see a turnoff to the right called Copp Road. About ½ mile later, turn left onto Mauna Place. Here you can visit the **University of Hawaii's Kula Experimental Station.** The station planted the first protea here in the mid-'60s and since then has gained the reputation for being the foremost protea research and development facility.

Within the gates, you'll see as many as 300 varieties of the exotic bloom, most with names to match: Rickrack Banksia, Veldfire Sunburst, Pink Mink, Blushing Bride, and Safari Sunset, to name just a few. You can talk to the growers to find out more about the plants, which were brought to Maui from Australia in 1965 by Dr. Philip Parvin, a University of Hawaii horticulture professor. Then you can proceed to one of Upcountry Maui's many commercial outlets and buy your favorite blooms. *Mauna Pl. in Upcountry Maui, tel. 808/878-1213. Admission free. Open weekdays 7-3:30, but you must stop at the office and sign a sheet releasing the station from any liability. You'll then be given a map to help you find your way.*

39 Retrace your steps to Kula Highway and, again, head toward Kahului. In about 4 miles, you'll come to the town of **Pukalani**, essentially an Upcountry bedroom community for Kahului. If you're pressed for time, this is the point from which you can take Highway 37 back to Kahului.

40 Otherwise, take a right onto Highway 400, which you'll find right in Pukalani, and head toward the *paniolo* (Hawaiian cowboy) village of **Makawao**. This tiny town was settled long ago by Portuguese immigrants who were brought to Maui to work the sugar plantations. After their contracts ran out, many of them moved Upcountry, where their descendants now work the neighboring Haleakala and Ulupalakua ranches. Once a year on the Fourth of July, the paniolos come out in force for the Makawao rodeo.

Time Out One of Makawao's most famous landmarks is **Komoda Store & Bakery** (3674 Baldwin Ave., tel. 808/572-7261), where you can get a delicious cream puff. They sell hundreds each day, as well as offering all the other trappings of a general store.

Besides the annual rodeo, Makawao also provides an opportunity to browse through unusual shops. You can find casual attire at **Collections** (3677 Baldwin Ave., tel. 808/572-0781); original children's toys and books at **Maui Child Toys & Books** (3643 Baldwin Ave., tel. 808/572-2765); and trinkets, souvenirs, and collectibles at **Goodies** (3633 Baldwin Ave., tel. 808/572-0288) or **Coconut Classics** (3647 Baldwin Ave., tel. 808/572-7103). **Glassman Galleries** (3682 Makawao Ave., tel. 808/572-0395) is the newest enterprise of Barbara Glassman, who brings us Maui Art Tours (*see* Guided Tours, above).

From Makawao, it's a short drive down toward the ocean on Baldwin Avenue to the Hana Highway. Make a left on the Hana Highway to head back to Kahului.

Tour 4: The Road to Hana

Numbers in the margin correspond with points of interest on the Exploring Maui map.

Don't let anyone tell you the Hana Highway is impassable, frightening, or otherwise unadvisable. Because of all the hype, you're bound to be a little nervous approaching it for the first time. But once you try it, you'll wonder if maybe there's somebody out there making it sound tough just to keep out the hordes. Certainly the road is challenging, spanning some 55 miles of turns and bridges. But it's not a grueling, all-day drive. The road isn't a freeway, but it has been resurfaced to make it a pleasant drive.

41 Start your trip to Hana in the little town of **Paia** by having breakfast at one of the restaurants that line the main street. **Charley's** (142 Hana Hwy., tel. 808/579–9453) is recommended; you can get a good meal here and watch the locals go by. We suggest you also stop at **Picnics** (30 Baldwin Ave., tel. 808/579–8021) to buy a lunch for the road.

If you want to do some shopping as well, Paia is a friendly little town. You can find clothing and keepsakes in shops run by retailers who'll stop and chat, ask where you're from, and, most likely, give you their card in case something doesn't fit or you'd like to return. Here you'll find artists, windsurfers, and some folks who've lived in these parts all their lives.

Paia was once a sugar-growing enclave, an operation complete with a mill and plantation camps. Shops opened by shrewd immigrants quickly sprouted to serve the workers, who probably found it easier to buy supplies near home. The town boomed during World War II when the Marines set up camp nearby. After the war, however, sugar grower Alexander & Baldwin closed its Paia operation, many workers moved on, and the town's population began to dwindle. Many residents took off for the new city of Kahului, where they were able to purchase their own homes.

In the 1960s, Paia became a hippie town as dropouts headed for the sunny shores of Maui to open ethnic shops, bizarre galleries, and unusual eateries. By the late 1970s, windsurfers had **42** discovered nearby **Hookipa Beach,** and soon Paia was the windsurfing capital of the world. You can see this in the youth of the town and in the budget inns that have cropped up to offer cheap accommodations to those who windsurf for a living. Paia is certainly a fun place.

As you begin your drive to Hana, remember that many people—mostly those who live in Hana—make this trip frequently. You'll recognize them because they're the ones who'll be zipping around every curve as if they had a death wish. They don't; they've just seen this so many times before that they don't care to linger. With stops, this drive should take you between two and three hours. Locals will do it in about 45 minutes. Pull over and let them pass.

About 10 miles from Paia, the famous road really begins to twist and turn (as it will for the next 40 miles or so). About 3 miles later, you'll come to the first of the Hana Highway's approximately 65 bridges. All along this stretch of road, waterfalls are abundant. There are plenty of places to pull off and park; all are ideal spots to stop and take a picture. You'll want to plan on doing this a few times, as the road's curves make driving without a break difficult. When it's raining (which is often), the drive is particularly beautiful: there are waterfalls everywhere.

43 As you drive on, you'll pass the small villages of **Huelo,** with its two quaint churches, and **Kailua,** home to Alexander & Baldwin's irrigation employees. At about mile marker 11, you can **44** stop at the bridge over **Puohokamoa Stream,** where there are more pools and waterfalls. If you walk up to the left of the first pool, you'll find a larger pool and waterfalls. Picnic tables are available at Puohokamoa Stream, so many people favor this as a stopping point.

④⑤ If you'd rather stretch your legs *and* use a flush toilet, continue on another mile to the **Kaumahina State Wayside Park,** which has a picnic area and a lovely overlook to the Keanae Peninsula. Hardier souls can camp here with a permit. *Admission free. No set hours.*

④⑥ A mile past the park, you'll see an enormous valley to your right. This is **Honomanu Valley,** carved by erosion during Haleakala's first dormant period. At the canyon's head, there are 3,000-foot cliffs and a 1,000-foot waterfall, but don't try to reach them. There's not much of a trail, and what does exist is practically impassable.

④⑦ Another 4 miles brings you to the **Keanae Arboretum,** where you can admire many plants and trees that are now considered native to Hawaii. The meandering Piinaau Stream adds a graceful touch to the arboretum and provides a swimming pond besides. You can take a fairly rigorous hike from the arboretum, if you can find the trail at one side of the large taro patch. You have to be careful not to lose the trail once you're on it. A lovely forest waits at the end of the hike. *Admission free. No set hours.*

④⑧ Near mile marker 17, you'll find the **Keanae Overlook.** From here, you'll notice the patchwork-quilt effect the taro farms create below. The ocean provides a dramatic backdrop, while in the other direction you have some awesome views of Haleakala through the foliage. This is a good spot for photos.

Coming up is the **halfway mark to Hana.** If you've had enough scenery, this is as good a time as any to turn around and head back to civilization. The scenery from here is essentially the same. Once you get to Hana, you can't expect a booming city. It's the road that's the draw. Diehards will want to stick with us.

Time Out At about mile marker 20, you can pull over at **Uncle Harry's** (tel. 808/248–7019), a refreshment stand run by Uncle Harry Mitchell. Uncle Harry and his family also have souvenirs for sale, and they've opened a small museum next door, including a grass house to demonstrate how their ancestors lived. The Mitchells have some Hawaiian food available, as well as fruit, home-baked breads, and beverages.

---

④⑨ Continue on from mile marker 20 for about ¾mile to **Wailua Lookout.** From the parking lot, you can see Wailua Canyon, but you'll have to walk up steps to get a view of Wailua Village. The landmark in Wailua Village is a church made of coral, built in 1860. Once called St. Gabriel's Catholic Church, the current Our Lady of Fatima Shrine has an interesting legend surrounding it; as the story goes, a storm washed just enough coral up onto the shore to build the church, but then took any extra coral back to sea.

⑤⓪ Another ½ mile, and you'll hit the best falls on the entire road to Hana. **Waikane Falls** are not necessarily bigger or taller than the other falls, but they're dramatic just the same. That's partly because the water is not diverted for sugar irrigation; the taro farmers in Wailua need all the runoff. Here is another good spot for photos.

About 9 miles past the Wailua Lookout, or at about mile marker 25, you'll see a road that heads down toward the ocean and the

51 village of **Nahiku.** This was a popular spot in ancient times, providing a home to hundreds of natives. Now Nahiku's population numbers about 80, consisting mostly of native Hawaiians and some back-to-the-land types. Like so many other Hawaiian villages, Nahiku was once a plantation town. A rubber grower planted trees there in the early 1900s. The experiment didn't work out, so Nahiku was essentially abandoned.

52 As you continue on toward Hana, you'll pass **Waianapanapa State Park,** which has state-run cabins where you can stay with a permit for between $14 and $30 a night, depending on the number of people (*see* Sports and Fitness, below). The park is right on the ocean, and it's a lovely spot to picnic, hike, or swim. An ancient burial site is located nearby, as well as a heiau, or temple. Waianapanapa also boasts one of Maui's only black-sand beaches and some caves for adventurous swimmers to explore. *Hana Hwy., tel. 808/248-8061. Admission free. No set hours.*

53 Closer to Hana, you'll come to **Helani Gardens,** a 60-acre enclave of plants collected and grown by Hana native Howard Cooper. Cooper is the crusty old guy you'll find wandering the place or hanging out in his treehouse. His wife, Nora, is editor of the *Maui News* in Kahului, but Howard just couldn't bear to leave his beloved Hana, so Nora commutes. Howard's philosophy of life crops up all over the garden in delightful, hand-painted signs. A tour of Helani Gardens is a self-guided one, but if Howard's around, he'll be glad to show you his favorite plants. *No street address; you can write to Helani Gardens, Box 215, Hana 96713, tel. 808/248-8274. Admission: $2 adults, $1 children 6-16. Open daily (weather permitting) 10-4.*

54 **Hana** is just minutes away from Helani Gardens. It's a blink-and-you'll-miss-it kind of place, with only a couple of roads and

55 clusters of houses. In Hana, a high spot is the **Hotel Hana-Maui** (Hana Hwy., tel. 808/248-8211), one of the best hotels in the state—if not the world (*see* Lodging, below). The famous **Hasegawa's Store** (Hana Hwy.) burned down in late 1990, but Harry Hasegawa promises the old general store that stocked everything from A to Z will be back in business soon.

Time Out **Tutu's** (tel. 808/248-8224) is a snack shop down by the bay. Aside from the Hotel Hana-Maui and its two eating establishments, this is the only place for a meal in the entire town. Although nothing is fancy here (burgers are the typical fare), the prices are lower than those at the hotel restaurants. You'll also get a view of fishing boats bringing in their catch in the late afternoon.

As you wander around Hana, keep in mind that this is a company town. Although sugar was once the mainstay of Hana's economy, the last plantation shut down in the 1940s. In 1946, rancher Paul Fagan built the Hotel Hana-Maui and stocked the surrounding pastureland with cattle. Suddenly, it was the ranch and its hotel that were putting food on the most tables.

The Cross you'll see on the hill above the hotel was put there in memory of Fagan. After Fagan died in the mid-1960s, ranch-and-town ownership passed into the hands of 37 shareholders, most of whom didn't care about their property. Then the Rosewood Corporation came along and purchased most of Hana's valuable land. Owned by Caroline Hunt, the company put megamillions into restoring the Hotel Hana-Maui and began teaching the *paniolos* (cowboys) all the latest techniques in grazing and breeding. Recently, however, Rosewood sold its Hana holdings to a Japanese company which appointed Sheraton as manager. No news is available on the resulting changes.

Because of the town's size, most of the townspeople are the hands-on suppliers of the services and amenities that make hotel guests happy. Moreover, many locals have worked at the hotel for years; a fascinating family tree that hangs near the lobby shows the relationships of all the employees. If you're at all adventurous, you'll no doubt be able to talk to several of the people who live and work in Hana. They're candid, friendly, and mostly native Hawaiian—or at least born and raised in Hana.

56 Once you've seen Hana, you might want to drive past the town for a dip in the pools at **Oheo Gulch.** Called the Piilani Highway once past Hana, the road that spans the 10 miles to the gulch is truly bad—rutted, rocky, and twisting. You're just sure you've passed the pools because the terrain is so awful, but don't give up. These refreshing pools are worth the drive. Oheo Gulch is often referred to as Seven Sacred Pools, but that is just a bit of promotional hype. There's nothing sacred here, unless you count sybaritic swimming as a religious pursuit, and the pools number far more than seven.

From the paved parking lot, you can walk a short way to the first of the pools. Rocks are available for sunbathing, and caves may be explored. In the spring and summer, it can get quite crowded here, and it doesn't even thin out when it rains.

57 A lot of people come this far just to see the **Grave of Charles Lindbergh,** the world-renowned aviator. Lindbergh chose to be buried here because he and his wife, Anne Morrow Lindbergh, spent a lot of time living in the area in a home they built. His grave is very difficult to spot, which is probably intentional. It's about a mile past Oheo Gulch on a road that goes toward the ocean. On this road you'll find **Hoomau Congregational Church**, next to which Lindbergh was buried in 1974. Remember, this is a churchyard, so be considerate and leave everything exactly as you found it.

Unless you've decided to drive completely around Maui and end up at Makena (which isn't advisable unless you have a four-wheel-drive vehicle), this is the place to turn around. You've seen just about all of Hana's high spots. The drive back isn't nearly as much fun, so you might want to plan on spending a night in Hana (*see* Lodging, below).

Maui for Free

Hale Paahao/Old Lahaina Prison. Here you can see the original coral-block walls that were once the jail for rowdy sailors and whalers. This prison was built between 1852 and 1854 by the prisoners themselves; the small, brown building looks like a chapel. The rock for the coral prison came from the walls of an old fort, which Hale Paahao replaced. *Prison Rd. just off Wainee St., Lahaina, tel. 808/661-3262. Open daily 9-5.*

Hale Pai/Old Print Shop. Located on the grounds of Lahainaluna School in Lahaina, this print house was opened in

1837 and put out the first Hawaiian-language newspaper. Founded by the missionaries, it now houses the Lahaina Restoration Foundation's extensive archival collection and exhibits depicting Maui's early whaling and missionary days. *At the mountain end of Lahainaluna Rd., Lahaina, tel. 808/661–3262. Open Mon.–Fri. 10–4.*

Hui Noeau Visual Arts Center. This nonprofit cultural center is set in the Upcountry town of Makawao in the old Baldwin estate. There are regular exhibitions, as well as audiovisual presentations. *2841 Baldwin Ave., Makawao, tel. 808/572–6560. Open daily 10–4.*

Jodo Mission. The Lahaina Jodo Mission Cultural Park is one of the town's busiest tourist attractions, sitting on a parcel of land called Puunoa Point just off Front Street near Mala Wharf. The park's centerpiece is the largest Buddha outside Japan, placed there to commemorate the arrival of the first Japanese immigrants in 1868. The park includes the shrine, graveyards, a crematorium, and an extensive outdoor meeting area. *12 Ala Moana, Lahaina, tel. 808/661–4304. No set hours.*

Lahaina Whaling Museum. Crazy Shirts' owner, Rick Ralston, has opened this repository of more than 800 pieces of whaling memorabilia in his Front Street store. His collection includes carved ivory, harpoons, and old photos. *865 Front St., tel. 808/661–4775. Open Mon.–Sat. 9 AM–10 PM, Sun. 9–9.*

Maui Zoological and Botanical Gardens (Kanaloa St. off Kaahumanu Ave., Kahului, tel. 808/243–7337). *See* Tour 2, above.

Muumuu Factory. Famous muumuu manufacturer **Hilo Hattie** advertises all over Maui. Owned by the same company that runs the Maui Tropical Plantation, Hilo Hattie stocks aloha wear made on the premises. The company will pick you up if you're staying in the Kaanapali or Lahaina area, or you can drive there yourself. Be forewarned that the clothing isn't much cheaper or better quality than what you'll find in the stores. *Lahaina Center, Lahaina, tel. 808/661–8457. Open daily 8:30–5.*

Pacific Brewery. Look for this operation on the grounds of the old Wailuku Sugar Mill. You can get 15-minute tours of this Maui Lager beer plant, which recently began shipping its product to the Mainland. The tour acquaints you with brewing and bottling techniques and ends with a taste test. *Imi Kala St., Wailuku, tel. 808/244–0396. Open weekdays 10–4.*

Reach Out to the Stars. Astronomy buffs can get their fill of stargazing at a unique nightly program at the Hyatt Regency Maui. A constellation slide show is followed by a look through giant binoculars and a deep-space telescope. The program is run by a real astronomer. *Hyatt Regency Maui's Lahaina Tower, 200 Nohea Kai Dr., Kaanapali, tel. 808/661–1234, ext. 3143. Wed.–Sun. 8 and 9 PM.*

Sandcastle Exhibition. Billy Lee is getting a reputation. The master sandcastle builder has set up his pails and shovels on the beach in front of 505 Front Street in Lahaina, and between 9 AM and sunset he sculpts whatever comes to mind—mermaids, castles, towers, lions, you name it.

Upcountry Protea Farm. On the slopes of Haleakala, Upcountry
Protea Farm grows exotic blossoms and offers views of the gardens to all who stop by. You can also purchase protea here, or
have them shipped home. *One mile off Hwy. 37, at the top of Upper Kimo Dr., tel. 808/878–2544. Open daily 8–4:30.*

Whalers Village Museum. On the shore at the Kaanapali Beach
Resort, this museum's exhibits explore whaling history. The
museum contains a 30-foot sperm whale skeleton, with information about whale biology, photos, and artifacts from 1825 to
1860. A video theater shows films, and an authentic whaling
boat is displayed in the outdoor pavilion. Lectures and special
tours are available. *2435 Kaanapali Pkwy., tel. 808/661–5992.
Open daily 9:30 AM–10 PM.*

What to See and Do with Children

Lahaina–Kaanapali & Pacific Railroad. Affectionately called
the Sugarcane Train, this choo-choo is Hawaii's only passenger
train. It's an 1890s-vintage railway that once shuttled sugar
but now moves sightseers between Kaanapali and Lahaina.
This quaint little attraction is a big deal for Hawaii but probably not much of a thrill for those more accustomed to trains.
The kids will like it. You can also get a package that combines a
ride and lunch in Lahaina or a historic Lahaina tour. *1½ blocks
north of the Lahainaluna Rd. stoplight on Honoapiilani Hwy.,
Lahaina, tel. 800/661–0080. Cost for round-trip ride: $10
adults, $5 children; one-way: $7 adults, $3.50 children. Open
daily 9–4.*

Maui Tropical Plantation. This visitor attraction used to be a
huge sugarcane field, but when Maui's once-paramount crop
declined severely in importance, a group of visionaries decided
to open an agricultural theme park. The 120-acre preserve now
ranks as Hawaii's third most popular tourist attraction. Located on Highway 30 just outside Wailuku, the plantation offers a
30-minute tram ride through its fields with an informative narration of growing processes and plant types.

Kids will also probably enjoy a historical-characters exhibit, as
well as fruit-testing, coconut-husking, and lei-making demonstrations and bird shows. There's a restaurant on the property
and a souvenir shop that sells fruits and vegetables. At night,
the Maui Tropical Plantation features a country barbecue. *On
Honoapiilani Hwy. right outside Wailuku toward Kaanapali,
tel. 808/244–7643. Admission free to the Marketplace; cost of
narrated tour, $8 adults, $3 children 6–12. Open daily 9–5.*

Whale-watching. Appealing to both children and adults, whale-watching is one of the most exciting activities in the United
States. During the right time of year on Maui—between December and April—you can see whales breaching and blowing
just offshore. The humpback whales' attraction to Maui is legendary. More than half the North Pacific's humpback population winters in Hawaii, as they've been doing for years. At one
time, thousands of the huge mammals existed, but the world
population has dwindled to about 1,500. In 1966, they were put
on the endangered-species list, which restricts boats and airplanes from getting too close.

Experts believe the humpbacks keep returning to Hawaiian
waters because of the warmth. Winter is calving time for the

behemoths, and the whale babies, born with little blubber, probably couldn't survive in the frigid Alaskan waters. No one has ever seen a whale give birth, but the experts studying whales off Maui know that calving is their main winter activity, since the one- and two-ton babies suddenly appear while the whales are in residence.

Quite a few operations run whale-watching excursions off the coast of Maui. This allows you to get a closer view; it gives the whale a better vantage point, too. Sometimes, in fact, a curious whale can get so close that it makes the passengers downright nervous. **Pacific Whale Foundation** (Kealia Beach Plaza, Kihei 96753, tel. 808/879–8811) pioneered whale-watching back in 1979 and now runs two boats.

Also offering whale-watching in season are the following: **Ocean Activities Center** (1325 S. Kihei Rd., Suite 212, Kihei 96753, tel. 808/879–4485); **Leilani Cruises** (505 Front St., Suite 225, Lahaina 96761, tel. 808/661–8397); **Captain Zodiac Raft Expeditions** (Box 1776, Lahaina 96761, tel. 808/667–5351); **Seabern Yachts** (Box 1022, Lahaina 96767, tel. 808/661–8110); and **Trilogy Excursions** (Box 1121, Lahaina 96767, tel. 808/661–4743). Ticket prices average about $30 adults, $15 children.

Off the Beaten Track

Kaupo Road. This stretch of road beyond Charles Lindbergh's grave is located near where the pavement stops 10 miles past Hana. Kaupo Road is rough, with more than a few miles of rocky, one-lane terrain not unlike that of the moon. Drop-offs plunge far down to the sea and washouts are common. It's a beautiful drive, however, and probably the closest to Old Hawaii you'll find. Along the way, the little Kaupo Store, about 15 miles past Hana, sells a variety of essential items, such as groceries, fishing tackle, and hardware; it's also a good place to stop for a cold drink. You'll also pass the renovated Hui Aloha Church, a tiny, wood-framed structure surrounded by an old Hawaiian graveyard. You might want a four-wheel-drive vehicle for this road. You'll eventually wind up near Makena.

Maui Swap Meet. The Maui Swap Meet flea market is the biggest bargain on Maui, with crafts, gifts, souvenirs, fruits, flowers, jewelry, antiques, art, shells, and lots more. *At the Kahului Fairgrounds, Hwy. 35, just off Puunene Ave. Admission: 50¢. Open Sat. 8–1.*

Yee's Orchard. If you're up for a little local shopping, look for Wilbert Yee's Orchard, near the Azeka Shopping Center (1280 S. Kihei Rd.) in Kihei. The Yee family has farmed the same 20-acre plot for more than half a century, raising mangoes, papayas, bananas, guavas, and tomatoes. You can also purchase certain livestock, such as chickens and peacocks. *Open Wed. 10–4 and Sun. 9–5.*

4 Shopping

Maui is not the place to go if you're in a serious shopping mood, but you can have fun browsing through the little stores that line Front Street in Lahaina or the boutiques packed into the major resort hotels. In all fairness, Maui does have three major shopping malls, in Kahului and Lahaina.

No matter if you head for the mall or opt for the boutiques hidden around the Valley Isle, one thing you should have no problem finding is clothing made in Hawaii. The Hawaiian garment industry is now the state's third-largest economic sector, after tourism and agriculture.

Maui has an abundance of locally made arts and crafts in a range of prices. In fact, a group that calls itself Made on Maui exists solely to promote the products of its members—items that range from pottery and paintings to Hawaiian teas and macadamia caramel corn. Made on Maui has a booth at the Kaahumanu Shopping Center, or you can identify the group by its distinctive Haleakala logo. Maui also boasts plenty of food choices besides the usual pineapple or macadamia nuts. Maui onions, protea, and potato chips are only a few of the possibilities.

Business hours for individual shops on the island are usually 9–5, seven days a week. Shopping centers tend to stay open later (until 9 on certain days).

Shopping Centers

Maui now has three major shopping centers: the Kaahumanu Center in Kahului, and the Lahaina Cannery Shopping Center and Lahaina Center in Lahaina. Newest of the three is the Lahaina Center, which opened in mid-1990.

Kaahumanu Center, in the heart of Kahului, takes up an entire block and boasts more than 60 shops and restaurants. The mall also has free parking. Its anchor stores are **Liberty House** (tel. 808/877–3361), **Sears** (tel. 808/877–2221), and the popular Japanese retailer **Shirokiya** (tel. 808/877–5551). Shirokiya's owners came to Hawaii long before the recent influx of Japanese businesses; their store is worth visiting for its electronic gadgets and other Japanese specialties.

Kaahumanu Center has other interesting shops, including the **Center for Performing Plants** (tel. 808/877–3655), which stocks a variety of greenery; **Lace Secrets** (tel. 808/871–6207), one of Maui's best lingerie stores; and the **Coffee Store** (tel. 808/871–6860), the place for a rich cup of java and good conversation. You can also find such recognizable Mainland stores as **Casual Corner, Kay-Bee Toys,** and **Radio Shack.** *Kaahumanu Center, 275 Kaahumanu Ave., Kahului, tel. 808/877–3369. Open Mon.–Wed. and Sat. 9–5:30, Thurs. and Fri. 9–9, Sun. 10–3.*

Time Out   While shopping at Kaahumanu Center, stop at **Ma-Chan's Okazu-ya** (tel. 808/877–7818), a delicatessen-like place where you can choose from Japanese snacks displayed behind a glass case. Dishes consist of bite-size portions of food, such as fish and rice, as well as chopped steak and chicken cutlets. The service here is friendly.

Lahaina Cannery Shopping Center is set in a building reminiscent of an old pineapple cannery. Unlike many shopping

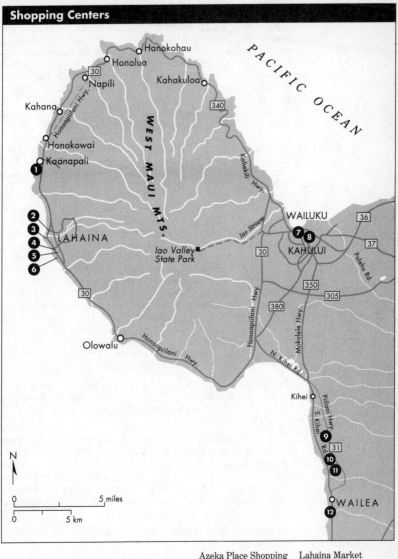

Shopping Centers

Azeka Place Shopping Center, **9**

505 Front Street, **6**

Kaahumanu Center, **7**

Kamaole Shopping Center, **10**

Lahaina Cannery Shopping Center, **2**

Lahaina Market Place, **4**

Lahaina Center, **3**

Maui Mall Shopping Center, **8**

Rainbow Mall, **11**

Wailea Shopping Village, **12**

Whalers Village, **1**

The Wharf Cinema Center, **5**

centers in Hawaii, the Lahaina Cannery isn't open-air; it is air-conditioned. The center has some 50 shops, including **Arabesque Maui** (tel. 808/667–5337), with classy fashions for women; **Dolphin Galleries** (tel. 808/661–5000), featuring sculpture, paintings, and other Maui artwork; **Superwhale** (tel. 808/661–3424), with a good selection of children's tropical wear; and **Kite Fantasy** (tel. 808/661–4766), one of the best kite shops on Maui. *Lahaina Cannery Shopping Center, 1221 Honoapiilani Hwy., Lahaina, tel. 808/661–5304. Open daily 9:30–9:30.*

Time Out **Sir Wilfred's** (tel. 808/667–1941) at the Lahaina Cannery is a charming spot to stop for coffee and croissants. The little eatery, a branch of a similar place in Central Maui, also sells tobacco and other gift items.

In West Maui, Lahaina has several shopping centers besides the Cannery. The newly opened **Lahaina Center** (corner of Front and Papalaua Sts.) houses the newest **Hard Rock Cafe** (900 Front St., tel. 808/667–7400) and several small shops. The **Wharf Cinema Center** (658 Front St., tel. 808/661–8748) boasts 31 air-conditioned shops and restaurants within a wooden building. Smaller centers include **505 Front Street** (tel. 808/667–2514), with its New England–style architecture, and **Lahaina Market Place** (corner of Front St. and Lahainaluna Rd., tel. 808/667–2636), a brick-paved area with 14 quality boutiques and eateries. North of Lahaina, at the Kaanapali Beach Resort, the upscale **Whalers Village** (2435 Kaanapali Pkwy., Kaanapali, tel. 808/661–4567) combines a shopping mall with a museum and has 31 galleries, shops, and restaurants.

In Central Maui, Kahului has one other large shopping center besides the Kaahumanu Center—the **Maui Mall Shopping Center** (corner of Kaahumanu and Puunene Aves., tel. 808/877–5523), with 33 stores.

In East Maui, Kihei offers the large and bustling **Azeka Place Shopping Center** (1280 S. Kihei Rd., tel. 808/879–4449) and the smaller **Kamaole Shopping Center** (2463 S. Kihei Rd., tel. 808/879–5233) and **Rainbow Mall** (2439 S. Kihei Rd., tel. 808/879–6144). South of Kihei, the Wailea Resort has the **Wailea Shopping Village** (tel. 808/879–4474), with 25 gift shops, boutiques, and restaurants.

For specific stores within shopping centers, consult the categories below.

Art

Maui has more art per square mile than any other Hawaiian Island—maybe more than any other U.S. county. Artists love Maui, and they flock there to live and work. There are artists' guilds and co-ops, as well as galleries galore. Moreover, the town of Lahaina hosts Art Night every Friday starting at 6; galleries open their doors, musicians stroll the streets, and Chinese lions parade along the main drag.

The **Old Jail Gallery,** located in the basement of the old Lahaina Court House (649 Wharf St., across the street from the Pioneer Inn and Lahaina Harbor), sells work by artists who belong to the Lahaina Arts Society (tel. 808/661–0111). The artists range from watercolorists to specialists in oil and sculpture. Down the street, **Sunset Galleries** (758 Front St., Lahaina, tel. 808/667–9112 and 156 Lahainaluna Rd., Lahaina, tel. 808/661–3371) has exclusive rights in Hawaii to sell the work of famous American Indian artist R. C. Gorman, among other artwork. Gorman's languid Navajo women have often been compared to the native Hawaiian lasses painted by island artist Pegge Hopper.

As for exclusivity, **Wyland Galleries** (697 Front St., Lahaina, tel. 808/661–7099; 711 Front St., Lahaina, tel. 808/667–2285; 136 Dickenson St., Lahaina, tel. 808/661–0590) is the only Maui shop to sell the work of Wyland, the marine artist whose favorite technique is a simultaneous look at scenes from under and above the water. **Coast Gallery** in the Maui Inter-Continental Wailea (3700 Wailea Alanui Dr., Wailea, tel. 808/879–2301) has an attractive selection of marine-related paintings and sculptures by such well-known artists as Richard Pettit, George Sumner, and Robert Lyn Nelson.

A popular Maui art enclave, **Village Gallery,** now has three locations—one in Lahaina (120 Dickenson St., tel. 808/661–4402), one at the Lahaina Cannery Shopping Center (tel. 808/661–3280), and one in the Embassy Suites (104 Kaanapali Shores Pl., tel. 808/667–5115) —featuring such local artists as Betty Hay Freeland, Wailehua Gray, and Margaret Bedell. **Lahaina Galleries** has three locations (728 Front St., Lahaina, tel. 808/667–2152; Whalers Village, Kaanapali Beach Resort, tel. 808/661–5571; Kapalua Resort, tel. 808/669–0202). One of the most interesting galleries on Maui is the **Maui Crafts Guild** (43 Hana Hwy., Paia, tel. 808/579–9697), on the road to Hana. Set in a two-story wooden building alongside the highway, the Guild is crammed with work by local artists; the best pieces are the pottery and sculpture. Upstairs, antique kimonos and batik fabric are on display.

If you want to buy directly from the artist, you can visit these gallery/studios: In Paia, near Dillon's Saloon (89 Hana Hwy.), lies the alleyway to **Eddie Flotte's Gallery** and studio (83 Hana Hwy., tel. 808/579–9641), where the young artist sells his watercolors that document the sagging town and its people. Flamboyant Italian artist Piero Resta has his **Resta Studios** (313 W. Kuiaha Rd., tel. 808/575–2203) in an old warehouse in the Upcountry town of Haiku. Visiting Resta is an experience in itself, but call first. Macario Pascual also allows visitors to his **Pascual Art Studio/Gallery** (551 Wainee St., Lahaina, tel. 808/667–6166).

Clothing

Aloha Wear   To find the kind of aloha wear, such as colorful shirts and muumuus, worn most by the people who live year-round on Maui, check out **Liberty House.** The store has six locations on the island, including shops in the Maui Marriott, Stouffer Wailea, and Maui Inter-Continental hotels and in Azeka Place Shopping Center (1280 S. Kihei Rd.) in Kihei, Whalers Village (2435 Kaanapali Pkwy.) in the Kaanapali Beach Resort, and Kaahumanu Center in Kahului. The largest Liberty House store is the one at Kaahumanu Center (tel. 808/877–3361).

Also in the Kaahumanu Center, **Sears** (tel. 808/877–2221) sells some decent muumuus and aloha shirts, as does **Andrade,** with its authentic, high-quality aloha wear in several hotel locations, including the Royal Lahaina, Sheraton Maui, Kapalua Bay, Maui Marriott, and Maui Inter-Continental. **Reyn's,** at the Kapalua Bay Hotel (tel. 808/669–5260) and the Lahaina Cannery Shopping Center (tel. 808/661–5356), and **Watumull's** (tel. 808/661–0528), at the Lahaina Market Place, also have tasteful selections. **Islandwear on the Beach** (505 Front St., Lahaina, tel. 808/661–8897) has choice selections from such Hawaiian-wear clothiers as Reyn Spooner and Malia.

If you want something a bit more brazen—as in louder prints; definitely not what the locals would wear, but something that might work better at a wild party at home—try **Island Muumuu Works** (180 Dickenson St., Lahaina, tel. 808/661–5360; and Maui Mall Shopping Center, corner of Kaahumanu and Puunene Aves., Kahului, tel. 808/871–6237). Also visit **Luana's,** with two Lahaina locations (869 Front St., tel. 808/667–2275; and 658 Front St., at the Wharf, tel. 808/661–0651), as well as the **Maui Muumuu Factory** (111 Hana Hwy., tel. 808/871–6672). Prices are generally cheaper at the abovementioned outlets.

Designer Fashions   Again, you can't go wrong at Liberty House, especially at its three designer-wear boutiques, called **Collections by Liberty House.** They're located at the Hyatt Regency and the Westin Maui, both in Kaanapali, and at the Maui Prince in Makena. **Silks Kaanapali** (tel. 808/667–7133), at the Whalers Village, is a delightful little shop that features hand-painted silk and exotic fashions from the Orient. **Brendi** (tel. 808/661–7113) at the Westin Maui, has a large selection of designer fashions, as does **Miki's Boutique** (tel. 808/879–3181), at the Wailea Shopping Village.

Resort Wear   You can find lots of casual, easygoing clothes at Liberty House or any of the hotel shops. Whalers Village in the Kaanapali Beach Resort has several good resort-wear shops, including **Foreign Intrigue** (tel. 808/667–6671) and **Paradise Clothing** (tel. 808/661–4638).

You can also wander along Front Street in Lahaina and poke through some of the shops that are tucked in along the way. For example, at the Lahaina Market Place, on the corner of Lahainaluna Road and Front Street, there's **Donna's Designs** (tel. 808/667–1952); **Island Casuals** (tel. 808/667–9156); and **Apparels of Pauline** (tel. 808/661–4774), which features hand-painted clothing by Maui designers. Look for **Joani's Boutique** (tel. 808/661–5588) and **Imports International** (tel. 808/661–8987), both in Wharf Cinema Center (658 Front St.).

In Paia, **Tropical Emporium** (104 Hana Hwy., tel. 808/579–8032) is one of the best resort-wear shops. At the hotels, you'll find your best bets at **Judges' Beyond the Reef at the Sugar Beach Resort** (145 N. Kihei Rd., Kihei, tel. 808/879–2979) and **Tahiti Imports** (tel. 808/661–4138) at the Sheraton-Maui.

Although stores for women's resort wear are easy to find on Maui, stores for men's resort wear are scarcer. Some recommended shops for men's clothing are: **Chapman's,** at the Hyatt Regency (tel. 808/661–4121) and at the Wailea Shopping Village (tel. 808/879–3644); **Kramer's Men's Wear,** at the Lahaina Cannery Shopping Center (tel. 808/661–5377) and Kaahumanu Center (tel. 808/871–8671); and **Reyn's,** in Kapalua (tel. 808/669–5260).

Food

Many visitors to Hawaii opt to take home some of the local produce: pineapples, papayas, guavas, coconut, or Maui onions. You can find jams and jellies—some of them Made on Maui products—in a wide variety of tropical flavors. Cook Kwee's Maui Cookies have gained quite a following, as have Maui Potato Chips. Both are available in most Valley Isle grocery stores. Maui has just started growing its own macadamia trees—but it takes seven years before nuts can be harvested! Still, macadamia nuts are a favorite gift back home.

Remember that fresh fruit must be inspected by the U.S. Department of Agriculture, so it's safer to buy a box that's already passed muster. **Paradise Fruit** (1913 Kihei Rd., Kihei, tel. 808/879–1723) sells ready-to-ship pineapples, Maui onions, and coconuts, while **Take Home Maui** (121 Dickenson St., Lahaina, tel. 808/661–8067) will deliver produce free to the airport or your hotel.

Maui is also the only place in Hawaii that commercially produces its own wine. You can find bottles of Maui Blanc (a pineapple wine), Maui Blush, and Maui Brut-Blanc de Noirs Hawaiian Champagne in grocery stores, but you might want to take a drive into Upcountry Maui and visit the **Tedeschi Winery** (tel. 808/878–6058). There, you can taste before you buy. Let's face it, the ambience is better there, too. To find the winery, take Highway 37 from Kahului toward Haleakala. Continue for about 25 miles, through Pukalani and past the Kula Sanatorium.

Gifts

You may be looking for a unique gift—expensive and unlike anything already sitting on your recipient's dusty bookcase. On the grounds of the Kapalua Bay Hotel, look for two fine shops guaranteed to fit the bill: **By the Bay** (107 Bay Dr., Kapalua, tel. 808/669–5227), which specializes in shells, coral, and handcrafted jewelry; and **Distant Drums** (125 Bay Dr., Kapalua, tel. 808/669–5522), a boutique that has put together a collection of primitive arts and crafts. **Maui on My Mind** (tel. 808/667–5597) at the Lahaina Cannery Shopping Center offers fine arts and crafts made right on Maui. **Maui's Best,** with its three locations—Kaahumanu Center, Wailea Shopping Village, and its own Kahului Warehouse (tel. 808/877–4831)—also has a wide selection of locally made gifts.

An unusual shop that's a recent addition to the group is the **Ship Model Gallery** (505 Front St., Lahaina, tel. 808/669–5461) with an extensive line of nautical antiques and memorabilia. Owner Konrad Juestel is also an expert on scrimshaw.

For less-expensive gifts, try some of Maui's better souvenir shops, such as **F. W. Woolworth** (tel. 808/877–3934) in Kahului's Maui Mall and **Maui Gift & Jewelry Factory Outlet** (520 Keolani Pl., Kahului, tel. 808/871–8086).

Hawaiian Arts and Crafts

Some visiting shoppers are determined to buy only what they can't get anywhere else. Some of the arts and crafts native to Hawaii can be just the thing. Woods such as koa and milo grow only in certain parts of the world, and because of their increasing scarcity, prices are rising. In Hawaii, craftsmen turn the woods into bowls, trays, and jewelry boxes that will last for years. One of the best places to find Hawaiian crafts on Maui is in the Upcountry town of Haiku, at **John of Maui & Sons** (100 Haiku Rd., Haiku, tel. 808/575–2863). If you're driving east from Kahalui, you'll need to turn right up Baldwin Avenue in Paia and drive for about 15 minutes. This little family operation turns out some of the most exacting wood products in the Islands.

Quilts may not sound Hawaiian, but the way they're done in the 50th state is very different from anywhere else in the world. Missionaries from New England were determined to teach the natives their homespun craft, but—naturally—the Hawaiians adapted quilting to their own style. **Lahaina General Store** (829 Front St., Lahaina, tel. 808/661–0944) and **Tutu's Palaka** (76 Hana Hwy., Paia, tel. 808/579–8682) have a few of these precious coverlets.

If you're looking for a unique experience while you're shopping for Hawaiian-made crafts, try the **Maui Rehabilitation Center** (95 Mahalani, Wailuku, tel. 808/244–5502). You won't find the world's most expert craftsmanship, but the prices are reasonable and you can meet some local folks who are just breaking into this segment of the visitor industry.

Technically neither a Hawaiian art nor craft, the fabric produced by **The Island** (314 Ano St., Kahului, tel. 808/871–4450) nevertheless possesses a definite Hawaiian character. A group of well-known Maui artists have formed this textile company, applying its colorful designs to bolts of beautiful print fabric.

Jewelry

In Lahaina, a visit to **Claire the Ring Lady** (858-4 Front St., tel. 808/667–9288) can be a worthwhile jewelry-buying expedition. The somewhat eccentric craftswoman will make an original piece of jewelry for you while you wait. **Jack Ackerman's The Original Maui Divers** (640 Front St., tel. 808/661–0988) is a company that's been crafting gold and coral into jewelry for about 20 years. You can buy Hawaiian heirloom jewelry and tiny carved pendants from **Lahaina Scrimshaw** (tel. 808/661–3971) in the Lahaina Cannery Shopping Center or at two locations on Front Street. **Haimoff & Haimoff Creations in Gold** (tel. 808/669–5213), located at the Kapalua Resort, features the original work of award-winning jewelry designer Harry Haimoff, and **Olah Jewelers** (839 Front St., Lahaina, tel. 808/661– 4551) displays Australian black opal jewelry designed by Yvette and George Olah.

5 Beaches, Sports, Fitness

Beaches

Maui has more than 100 miles of coastline. Not all of this is beach, of course, but Maui's striking white crescents do seem to be around every bend. All of Hawaii's beaches are free and open to the public—even those that grace the front yards of fancy hotels—so you can feel free to make yourself at home on any one of them.

While they don't appear often, be sure to pay attention to any signs on the beaches. Warnings of high surf or rough currents should be noted. Before you seek shade under a swaying palm tree, watch for careening coconuts. Though the trades seem gentle, the winds are strong enough to knock the fruit off the trees and onto your head. Also be sure to diligently apply that sunscreen. Maui is closer to the equator than the beaches to which you're probably accustomed, so although you may think you're safe, take it from those who've gotten a beet-red burn in 30 minutes or less—you're not. Drinking alcoholic beverages on beaches in Hawaii isn't allowed.

West Maui boasts quite a few beach choices. If you start at the northern end of West Maui and work your way down the coast in a southerly direction, you'll find the following beaches:

D. T. Fleming Beach is one of West Maui's most popular beaches. This charming, mile-long sandy cove is better for sunbathing than for swimming, because the current can be quite strong. There are rest-room facilities, including showers; picnic tables and grills; and paved parking. *Take Hwy. 30 about 1 mi north of the Kapalua Resort.*

The lovely **Napali Beach** is located right outside the **Napili Kai Beach Club,** a popular little condominium for honeymooners. This sparkling white crescent makes a secluded cove perfect for strolling. No facilities are available here unless you're staying at the condo, but you're only a few miles south of Kapalua. *5900 Honoapiilani Hwy. From the upper highway, take the cutoff road closest to the Kapalua Resort.*

Honokowai Beach is a bust if you're looking for that classic Hawaiian stretch of sand. Still, kids will enjoy the rocks here that have formed a pool. This beach does have showers and picnic tables. *Across from the Honokowai Superette at 3636 Lower Honoapiilani Rd.*

Fronting the big hotels at Kaanapali is one of Maui's best people-watching spots, **Kaanapali Beach.** This is not the beach if you're looking for peace and quiet, but if you want lots of action, lay out your towel here. Cruises, windsurfers, and parasails exit off this beach while the beautiful people take in the scenery. Although no facilities are available, the nearby hotels have rest rooms. You're also close to plenty of shops and concessions. *Take any one of the three Kaanapali exits from Honoapiilani Hwy. Park at any of the hotels.*

South of Lahaina at mile marker 14 is **Olowalu Beach,** a secluded snorkeling haven. There's no parking here—except right on the road—and no facilities, but it's one of Maui's best sandy spots. With mask and fins, you'll see yellow tangs, parrot fish, and sometimes the state fish, the humuhumunu-kunukuapuaa. You can call it a humu, if you like.

Farther south of Olowalu, you'll find **Wailea's five crescent beaches,** which stretch for nearly 2 miles with relatively little interruption by civilization. Two hotels call Wailea home, with three condominiums now under construction. So far, the buildings haven't infringed on the beaches in a noticeable way. With any luck, the population boom won't affect this area either. Swimming is good here—the crescents protect the shoreline from rough surf. Few people populate these beaches—mostly guests of the nearby lodgings—which makes Wailea a peaceful haven.

Just south of Wailea is **Makena,** with two good beaches. **Big Beach** is 3,000 feet long and 100 feet wide. The water off Big Beach is fine for swimming and snorkeling. If you walk over the cinder cone at Big Beach, you'll reach **Little Beach,** which is used for nude sunbathing. Officially, nude sunbathing is illegal in Hawaii, but several bathers who've pushed their arrests through the courts have found their cases dismissed. Understand, though, that you take your chances if you decide to partake of a favorite local pastime at Little Makena.

The beaches in Central Maui are far from noteworthy, but if you're staying in the area, try **Kanaha Beach** in Kahului. A long, golden strip of sand bordered by a wide grassy area, this is a popular spot for windsurfers, joggers, and picnicking Maui families. Kanaha Beach has toilets, showers, picnic tables, and grills. *In Kahului, take Dairy Rd. toward the airport. At Koeheke, make a left and head toward Kahului Bay.*

If you want to see some of the world's finest windsurfers, stop at **Hookipa Beach** on the Hana Highway. The sport has become an art—and a career, to some—and its popularity was largely developed right at Hookipa. Waves get as high as 15 feet. This is not a good swimming beach, nor the place to learn windsurfing yourself, but plenty of picnic tables and barbecue grills are available. *About 1 mi past Paia on Hwy. 36.*

In East Maui, **Kaihalulu Beach** was once a favorite spot of privacy-seeking nudists. Now, however, Hana's red-sand beach has gotten a little less secluded as more people have discovered it, but this is still a gorgeous cove, with good swimming and snorkeling. To get there, start at the Hana Community Center at the end of Hauoli Road and walk along the outside of Kauiki Hill. The hike won't be easy, but it's worth the effort. No facilities are available.

Sports and Fitness

Participant Sports

Bicycling   Maui's roads are narrow, which can make bicycling a harrowing experience. Some visitors rent a bike just to ride around the resort where they're staying, but to go anywhere else requires getting on a two-lane highway. If it looks like something you'd like to try anyway, **A & B Moped Rental** (3481 Lower Honoapiilani Hwy., Lahaina, tel. 808/669–0027) is about your only choice. Bikes rent for $10 an hour.

Camping and Hiking   Like the other Hawaiian islands, Maui is riddled with ancient paths. These were the roads the Polynesians used to cross from one side of their island home to another. Most of these paths today are too difficult to find. But if you happen to stumble upon something that looks like it might have been a trail, chances are good it was used by the ancients.

In fact, most trails on Maui are not well marked. Only three areas have clearly marked trailheads. Luckily, they're some of the best hikes on the island.

In Maui's center, **Haleakala Crater** in Haleakala National Park is an obvious hiking haven, boasting several trails. As you drive to the top of the 10,023-foot dormant volcano on the Haleakala Highway, you'll first come to **Hosmer Grove,** less than a mile after you enter the park. This is a lovely forested area, with an hour-long nature trail. You can pick up a map at the trailhead and camp without a permit in the campground. There are six campsites, pit toilets, drinking water, and cooking shelters. There's also **Halemauu Trail,** near the 8,000-foot elevation. The walk to the crater rim is a grassy stroll, then it's a switchback trail nearly 2 miles to the crater floor. Nearly 4 miles from the trailhead, you'll find **Holua Cabin,** which you can reserve—at least three months in advance—through the National Park Service (Box 369, Makawao 96768, tel. 808/572–9306). Nearby, you can pitch a tent, but you'll need a permit that's issued on a first-come, first-served basis at Haleakala National Park Headquarters/Visitors Center (Haleakala Crater Rd., 7,000-ft elevation, tel. 808/572–9306. Open daily 7:30–4).

If you opt to drive all the way to the top of Haleakala, you'll find a trail called **Sliding Sands,** which starts at about the 10,000-foot elevation, descending 4 miles to the crater floor. The scenery is spectacular; it's colorful and somewhat like the moon. You can reach the abovementioned Holua Cabin in about 7 miles if you veer off to the left and out of the crater on the Halemauu Trail. If you continue on the Sliding Sands Trail, however, you'll come to **Kapalaoa Cabin** within about 6 miles, and at about 10 miles you'll hit **Paliku Cabin,** both also available from the park service with at least three months' notice. All three cabins have bunks, firewood, water, and a stove and are limited to 12 people. They can be reached in less than a day's walk. Paliku Cabin has tent camping nearby with toilets and drinking water. Tent permits, again, are issued at park headquarters on the day you want to use them.

Kaupo Gap is a trail you might want to use to hike out of Haleakala, but it will put you on the northeastern side of the island, along the Hana Highway. It begins at about 6,400 feet and descends through private ranch land. This is a rough trail—9 miles from Paliku Cabin to Highway 31—and hiking it can take as long as 10 hours. It's all downhill, which is particularly strenuous on already-tired legs and feet.

Maui's second hiking area, in East Maui, is called **Oheo Gulch.** The gulch is part of Haleakala National Park, but it's very different from the crater. That's because it's over on the Hana side of the park—which actually extends far beyond the mountain you see in the clouds. This is a lush, rainy, tropical area. You can reach Oheo Gulch by continuing on the Hana Highway about 10 miles past Hana. Oheo Gulch includes the Seven Pools, where the two major trails begin. The first trail is **Makahiku Falls,** a half-mile jaunt from the parking lot to an overlook. You can go around the barrier and get closer to the falls if you want. From here, you can continue on the second trail for another 1½ miles.

You'll dead-end at **Waimoku Falls.** There's camping in this area, with no permit required, although you can stay only three nights. Toilets, grills, and tables are available here, but no water.

Another camping and hiking area is located on the southern slope of Haleakala. Called **Polipoli Forest,** this place will remind you of a Walt Disney movie. It was once heavily forested, until cattle and goats chewed away most of the natural vegetation. Starting in about 1930, the government began a program to reforest the area, and soon redwoods, cedar, pine, and cypress took hold. Because of the elevation, it's a bit cooler here and sometimes wet and misty. But you'll appreciate the peace and quiet.

To reach the forest, drive on Highway 377 past Haleakala Road to Waipoli Road. Go up the hill until you reach the park. Next to the lot, you'll see a small campground and a cabin you can rent from the Division of State Parks (write far in advance for the cabin to: Box 1049, Wailuku 96793, tel. 808/244–4354; for the campground, you can wait until you arrive in Wailuku, then visit the State Parks office at 54 High St.). Once you're at Polipoli, there are three trails from which to choose.

The first trail you'll see is **Redwood Trail,** which starts at the camping area. The elevation here is about 6,200 feet, and the trail winds through groves of redwoods and pines until it ends near the ranger's cabin at about 5,300 feet. This hike will take about an hour.

For terrific views, try the **Haleakala Ridge Trail.** It's a fairly easy 1.6-mile hike along a semi-bare ridge. At the end, you'll find a small cave often used for shelter, including overnight camping. Take your camera, because you will walk along a ridge that boasts some of Hawaii's best scenery.

If you want to ascend a fairly rough and rocky path, try the **Upper Waiakoa Trail.** It begins at 6,400 feet and goes 7 miles, until you've reached a viewing point at 7,800 feet. This trail isn't an easy stroll, but you'll be rewarded with terrific vistas at the top.

Other areas around Maui are good for hiking, but they're a bit more difficult to find since trailheads aren't always marked. Look for these areas:

Iao Valley. Drive on Iao Valley Road west from the Central Maui town of Wailuku to reach this spot. Here, you can drive up to a lookout to see the famous Iao Needle. Go up the steps to the viewing point and climb over the railing on the left. Follow the dirt trail going upward. If you climb 2 miles, to a plateau behind the Iao Needle, you'll find some great views.

Waianapanapa State Park. This spectacular park is located right before you reach Hana town; you can camp here and take some hikes along the wild coastline. One trail leads from the park along the coast for 3 miles, ending at Hana Bay. Another heads in the opposite direction, past old burial sites. The park has 12 cabins—each with electricity, bathrooms, kitchens, two bedrooms, and linens—that rent for between $5 and $7 per person a night. These cabins must be reserved months in advance through the **Division of State Parks** (Box 1049, Wailuku 96793, tel. 808/244–4354). Campsites for 60 people are also available at Waianapanapa. You'll need a permit, but these sites are available free from the state by writing to the above address. At the campground, you'll find cold showers, flush toilets, drinking water, and cooking facilities.

Fitness Centers There are more fitness centers in hotels than anywhere else on Maui, and those will probably be the most convenient for you. At the Kaanapali Resort, the **Hyatt Regency** has a guests-only health spa with all the trimmings and daily aerobics classes; the **Maui Marriott** boasts a weights room and aerobics with a $3 charge for nonguests; and the **Westin Maui** has a health club with weights, aerobics, and massage. If you're a Westin guest, this is the best spa. At Wailea, both the Maui Inter-Continental and Stouffers offer aerobics daily.

Outside the resorts, the **Lahaina Nautilus Center** (180 Dickenson St., Suite 201, tel. 808/667-6100) has a complete fitness center as does **World Gym** (845 Wainee St., Lahaina, tel. 808/667-0422), which specializes in weights. The **Kahana Gym** (4310 Lower Honoapiilani Hwy., Kahana, tel. 808/669-7622) specializes in free weights. There are other clubs as well, but they are simply not convenient unless you want to drive to Kahului or Wailuku—about an hour from West Maui and 45 minutes from Wailea.

Golf How do you keep your mind on the game in a place like Maui? It's very hard, because you can't ignore the view. The island's three major resorts all have golf courses, each of them stunning. They're all open to the public as well.

The **Royal Kaanapali Golf Courses** (Kaanapali Beach Resort, Lahaina, tel. 808/661-3691) are two of Maui's most famous, due to television exposure. The layout consists of two 18-hole courses, which are each celebrities in their own right. The North Course was designed by Robert Trent Jones, Sr., while the South Course architect was Arthur Jack Snyder. Greens fees run about $90 for guests and nonguests.

The **Kapalua Golf Club** (300 Kapalua Dr., Lahaina, tel. 808/669-8044) has two 18-holers—the Village Course and the Bay Course—both designed by Arnold Palmer. Kapalua is also well known among television sports watchers. One of the Kapalua Bay Hotel owners is Mark Rolfing, who's made a name for himself as a producer of sporting events (he founded the Kapalua International) and as an announcer on ESPN. Rolfing, who's barely 40, started as a grease monkey in the cart barn. Greens fees at Kapalua are $75 for nonguests, $45 for guests. Carts go for $15 and clubs for $25.

The **Wailea Golf Club** (120 Kaukahi St., Wailea, tel. 808/879-2966) also has two courses—the Orange and the Blue—which were designed by Arthur Jack Snyder. In his design, the golf architect incorporated ancient lava-rock walls and *heiaus* (temples) for an even more unusual golfing experience. Greens fees are $105 for nonguests and $60 for guests.

The island's newest resort at Makena has a golf course as well, the lovely **Makena Golf Course** (5415 Makena Alanui Rd., Kihei, tel. 808/879-3344), designed by Robert Trent Jones, Jr. Of all the resort courses, this one is the most remote. At one point, golfers must cross a main road, but there are so few cars that this poses no problem. Greens fees are $100 per person, including a cart.

Maui has municipal courses as well, where the fees are lower. Be forewarned, however, that the weather can be cooler and wetter, while the locations may not be as convenient as you are used to at home. The **Waiehu Municipal Golf Course** (tel. 808/ 243–7400) is set on the northeast coast of Maui a few miles past Wailuku off Highway 340. Greens fees are $25; carts are $13. Up the hill from Kihei, the **Silversword Golf Course** (1345 Piilani Hwy., Kihei, tel. 808/874–0777) charges $50 including a cart.

Hang Gliding One company on Maui will strap wings on your back and let you jump off a cliff, but it insists on giving you lessons first. You can also try tandem flights, where an instructor handles all the flying and you just lie back and enjoy. Experienced hang gliders can leap off Haleakala Crater. Contact **Maui Soaring Supplies** (RR 2, Box 780, Kula, tel. 808/878–1271). Beginner lessons start at about $48.

Horseback Riding You have your choice here: You can take a one- or two-hour ride or you can opt for a daylong tour along scenic trails. **Pony Express Tours** (Box 535, Kula 96790, tel. 808/667–2200) charges $25 for an hour's ride on Haleakala Ranch or $120 for a full day. Also in East Maui, **Makena Stables** (7299–A S. Makena Rd., Kihei 96753, tel. 808/879–0244) offers, among other rides, a 5½hour winery tour with a catered lunch for $125. In West Maui, **Rainbow Ranch** (Box 10066, Lahaina 96761, tel. 808/669– 4991) charges $25 for an hour-long beginner's plantation ride; a three-hour picnic ride goes for $50. **Kaanapali Kau Lio** (Box 10656, Lahaina 96761, tel. 808/667–7896), another West Maui stable, offers a guided three-hour mountain ride above Kaanapali for $53; it also has a sunset ride for $67.

For a five-hour ride through an unspoiled Maui rain forest, streams, and a secluded waterfall, call **Adventures on Horseback** (Box 1771, Makawao 96768, tel. 808/242–7445 or 808/572– 6211). Mauian Frank Levinson takes only six riders at a time and provides a picnic lunch. This is a highly recommended way to go horseback riding, although you'll pay more than the standard hourly rate. The cost is $125.

Tennis The state's finest tennis facilities are at the **Wailea Tennis Club** (131 Wailea Ike Pl., Kihei, tel. 808/879–1958), often called "Wimbledon West" because of its grass courts; there are also 11 Plexipave courts and a pro shop. You'll pay between $10 and $12 an hour per person for the hard courts, and between $40 and $60 per court per hour for the grass numbers. At the Makena Resort, just south of Wailea, the **Makena Tennis Club** (5415 Makena Alanui Rd., Kihei, tel. 808/879–8777) has six courts. Rates are $5 per person per hour for guests, $8 for nonguests. After an hour, if there's space available, there's no charge.

Over on West Maui, the **Royal Lahaina Tennis Ranch** (2780 Kekaa Dr., tel. 808/661–3611 ext. 2296) in the Kaanapali Beach Resort offers 11 courts and a pro shop. Guests pay $6 a day per person, while nonguests are charged $9. The **Hyatt Regency Maui** (200 Nohea Kai Dr., Kaanapali, tel. 808/661–1234, ext. 3174) has five courts, with rentals and instruction. Courts go for $12 an hour for singles, $15 for doubles. Farther north, **Kapalua Tennis Garden** (100 Kapalua Dr., Kapalua, tel. 808/ 669–5677) serves the Kapalua Resort with 10 courts and a pro shop. You'll pay $9 a day if you're a guest, $10 if you're not.

There are other facilities around the island, usually one or two courts in smaller hotels or condos. Most of them, however, are open only to their guests. The best free courts are the five at the **Lahaina Civic Center** (1840 Honoapiilani Hwy., Lahaina, tel. 808/661-4685), near Wahikuli State Park; they're available on a first-come, first-served basis.

Water Sports   If fishing is your sport, Maui is the place for it. You'll be able to
Deep-Sea Fishing   throw in hook and bait for fish like *ahi* (yellowfin tuna), *aku* (a skipjack tuna), barracuda, bonefish, *kawakawa* (bonito), mahi-mahi, (a dolphin fish—*not* the mammal), Pacific blue marlin, *ono* (wahoo), and *ulua* (jack crevalle). On Maui, you can fish throughout the year, and you don't need a license.

Plenty of fishing boats run out of Lahaina and Maalaea harbors. If you charter a boat by yourself, expect to spend in the neighborhood of $600 a day. But you can share the boat with others who are interested in fishing the same day for about $100. While there are at least 10 companies running boats on a regular basis, these are the most reliable: **Finest Kind Inc.** (Box 10481, Lahaina 96767, tel. 808/661-0338), **Hinatea Sportfishing** (Slip 18/Lahaina Harbor, Lahaina 96761, tel. 808/667-7548), and **Luckey Strike Charters** (Box 1502, Lahaina 96767, tel. 808/661-4606). **Ocean Activities Center** (1325 S. Kihei Rd., Suite 212, Kihei 96753, tel. 808/879-4485 or 800/367-8047 ext. 448) can arrange fishing charters as well. You're responsible for finding your own transportation to the harbor.

Sailing   Because of its proximity to the smaller islands of Molokai, Lanai, Kahoolawe, and Molokini, Maui can provide one of Hawaii's best sailing experiences. Most sailing operations like to combine their tours with a meal, some throw in snorkeling or whale-watching, while others offer a sunset cruise. If you want to really sail—as opposed to cruising on a motorized catamaran or other vessel—try **Genesis Sailing Charters** (Box 10697, Lahaina 96761, tel. 808/667-5667), **Maui-Molokai Sea Cruises** (831 Eha St., Suite 101, Wailuku 96793, tel. 808/242-8777), **Sail Hawaii** (Box 573, Kihei 96753, tel. 808/879-2201), **Scotch Mist Charters** (Box 831, Lahaina 96767, tel. 808/661-0386), and **Seabern Yachts** (Box 1022, Lahaina 96767, tel. 808/661-8110).

Scuba Diving   Believe it or not, Maui is just as scenic underwater as it is above. In fact, some of the finest diving spots in Hawaii lie along the Valley Isle's western and southwestern shores. If you're a certified diver, you can rent gear at any Maui dive shop simply by showing your PADI or NAUI card. Unless you're familiar with the area, however, it's probably best to hook up with a dive shop for an underwater tour. Additionally, the only really decent shore dive is at Honolua Bay, a marine reserve above Kapalua Resort. The water is usually rough during the winter.

Popular Maui dive shops—stores that deal exclusively in the sale and rental of diving equipment, as well as lessons and certification—include **Capt. Nemo's Ocean Emporium** (150 Dickenson St., Lahaina, tel. 808/661-5555), **Central Pacific Divers** (780 Front St., Lahaina, tel. 808/661-8718), **Dive Maui** (Lahaina Market Place, Lahaina, tel. 808/667-2080), **Ed Robinson's Diving Adventures** (Box 616, Kihei, tel. 808/879-3584), and **Lahaina Divers** (710 Front St., Lahaina, tel. 808/667-7496). All provide equipment with proof of certification, as well as introductory dives for those who aren't certified. Introductory boat dives generally run about $60.

Dive shops have their own favorite spots, but we describe places below that we think are better than others. You can consult a dive shop near you for further information.

Cathedrals is a group of pinnacles off the nearby island of Lanai that rise from 60 feet to just below the water's surface. There are fascinating chambers that play games with the sun rays in beautiful ways; the chambers provide a home to moray eels, lobsters, and ghost shrimp, who keep the area well watched.

Mokuhooniki Rock lies off the east coast of nearby Molokai. During World War II, it was a military bombing target, so there are plenty of interesting artifacts to explore. Large pelagic fish hang around here, such as barracuda, gray reef sharks, and ulua.

In fact, there are pieces of military equipment for exploring in a couple of locations off Maui: a Sherman tank and landing craft in 60 feet of water off the shore of southwest Maui, and another Sherman tank at 80 feet off shore from the Makena Resort.

Snorkeling The same dive companies that take scuba aficionados on tours will take snorkelers as well—for a lot less money. One of Maui's most popular snorkeling spots can be reached only by boat: Molokini Crater, that little bowl of land off the coast of the Makena Resort. For about $55, you can spend the day at Molokini, with meals provided. **Ocean Activities Center** (1325 S. Kihei Rd., Suite 212, Kihei 96753, tel. 808/879–4485) does the best job with a Molokini tour, although other companies also do this tour.

You can also find some good snorkeling spots on your own. Specifically, secluded **Windmill Beach** (take Hwy. 30 3½ mi north of Kapalua, then turn onto the dirt road to the left) has a superb reef for snorkeling. A little more than 2 miles south, another dirt road leads to **Honolua Bay;** the coral formations on the right side of the bay are particularly dramatic. One beach south of the Kapalua Resort, you'll find **Napili Bay,** which is also quite good for snorkeling.

Almost the entire coastline from Kaanapali south to Olowalu offers fine snorkeling. Favorite sites include the area just out from the cemetery north of Wahikuli State Park, near the lava cone called **Black Rock,** on which Kaanapali's Sheraton Maui Hotel is built (tame fish will take bread from your hand there); and the shallow coral reef at **Olowalu** (south of Olowalu General Store).

The coastline from Kihei to Makena is also generally good for snorkeling. The best is found near the rocks of **Kamaole Beach III** in Kihei and the rocky fringes of Wailea's **Mokapu, Ulua, Wailea,** and **Polo** beaches.

Between Polo Beach and Makena Beach (shortly before the turnoff to Ulupalakua) lies **Five Caves,** where you'll find a maze of underwater grottoes below offshore rocks. This spot is recommended for experienced snorkelers only, since the tides can get rough. At Makena, the waters around the **Puu Olai** cinder cone provide great snorkeling.

If you need gear, **Snorkel Bob's** (5425 Lower Honoapiilani Rd., Napili, tel. 808/669–9603), in the Napili Village Hotel, will rent you a mask, fins, and snorkel, and throw in a carrying bag, map, and snorkel tips for $15 a week.

Surfing   Although on land it may not look as if there are seasons on Maui, the tides tell another story. In winter, the surf's up on the northern shores of the Hawaiian Islands, while summer brings big swells to the southern side. That means the near-perfect winter waves on Maui can be found at **Honolua Bay,** on the northern tip of West Maui. To get there, continue 2 miles north of D. T. Fleming Park on Highway 30 and take a left onto the dirt road next to a pineapple field; a path takes you to the beach.

Next best for surfing is **Hookipa Beach Park** (off Hwy. 36 a short distance east of Paia), where the modern-day sport began on Maui. This is the easiest place to watch surfing, because there are paved parking areas and picnic pavilions in the park. A word of warning: The guys who come here are pros, and if you're not, they may not take kindly to your getting in their way.

In summer, surf's up on the southern shores of **Maalaea Bay,** above Kihei, and **Lahaina.** Lahaina doesn't rival the winter sets at the other spots, and Maalaea's conditions can be inconsistent.

You can rent surfboards and boogie boards at many surf shops, such as **Indian Summer Surf Shop** (193 Lahainaluna Rd., Lahaina, tel. 808/661–3794); **Second Wind** (111 Hana Hwy., Kahului, tel. 808/877–7467); **Lightning Bolt Maui** (55 Kaahumanu Ave., Suite E, Kahului, tel. 808/877–3484); and **Ole Surfboards** (1036 Limahana Pl., Lahaina, tel. 808/661–3459).

Waterskiing   Only one company tows water-skiers off the coast of Maui: **Lahaina Water Ski** (104 Wahikuli Rd., Lahaina, tel. 808/661–5988). For $30 per 15 minutes for one person, $50 per 30 minutes for one to three people, or $90 an hour for one to five people, Lahaina Water Ski provides the boat, driver, and equipment.

Windsurfing   It's been more than 10 years since Hookipa Bay was discovered by boardsailors, but in those years since 1980, the windy beach 10 miles east of Kahului has become the windsurfing capital of the world. The spot boasts optimal wave-sailing wind and sea conditions and, for experienced windsurfers, can offer the ultimate experience. Other locations around Maui are good for windsurfing as well—Honolua Bay, for example—but Hookipa is absolutely unrivaled.

Even if you're a windsurfing aficionado, chances are good you didn't bring your equipment. You can rent it—or get lessons—from these shops: **Kaanapali Windsurfing School** (104 Wahikuli Rd., Lahaina, tel. 808/667–1964), **Maui Magic Windsurfing School** (520 Keolani Pl., Kahului, tel. 808/877–4816), **Ocean Activities Center** (1325 S. Kihei Rd., Kihei, tel. 808/879–4485), and **Maui Windsurfari** (Box 330254, Kahului, tel. 808/871–7766). Lessons range from $30 to $60 and can last anywhere from one to three hours. Equipment rental also varies—from no charge with lessons to $20 an hour. For the latest prices and special deals, it's best to call around once you've arrived.

Spectator Sports

Basketball   In late November, the **Maui Classic** holds court at the Lahaina Civic Center (tel. 808/669–6844) in a series of games. The Maui

Classic brings in such teams as the Michigan Wolverines, the Runnin' Rebels of Nevada–Las Vegas, and the Oklahoma Sooners for four days of preseason games. Call the Civic Center for exact dates and times.

Golf Tournaments Maui has a number of golf tournaments, many of which are televised on ESPN. Especially popular during the last two months of each year, Maui's golf tourneys are of professional caliber and worth watching. The **Isuzu Kapalua International Championship of Golf** held each November at the Kapalua Resort is the granddaddy of them all and now draws big names competing for a $600,000 purse. Also at Kapalua is the **Kirin Cup World Championship of Golf,** with teams representing the U.S. Professional Golf Association (PGA) tour, the European PGA tour, the Japan PGA Tour, and the Australia/New Zealand PGA tour. Golfing greats play on Kapalua's Bay Course for a $1.1 million purse each December. At Kaanapali, the **GTE Kaanapali Golf Classic** pits senior duffers in a battle for a $300,000 purse each December. Over in Wailea, the **Annual Asahi Beer Kyosan Golf Tournament** has a $100,000 purse, and the **LPGA Women's Kemper Open** moved from Kauai to Wailea starting with the February 1990 tournament. For more information on specific dates for all these tournaments, call Rolfing Productions, tel. 808/669–4844.

Windsurfing Not many places can lay claim to as many windsurfing tournaments as Maui. The Valley Isle is generally thought to be the world's preeminent windsurfing location, drawing board-sailing experts from around the globe who want to compete on its waves. In April, the **Marui/O'Neil Invitational** lures top windsurfers from at least a dozen countries to vie for a $30,000 purse. The **Hawaiian Pro-Am Speed Slalom Windsurfing Competition** and **Wailea Speed Crossing** take place in September, and the **Maui Grand Prix** and the **Aloha Classic Wave Sailing World Championships** are held in October. The **Junior World Wave Sailing Championships,** for kids under 18 from around the world, is in May. All events are held at Hookipa Bay, right outside the town of Paia, near Kahului.

6   Dining

Maui cuisine consists of a lot more than the poi and pineapple you'll find at a local luau. It's also more than the burgers and fries doled out at the ubiquitous fast-food chains that in some towns seem to post a store on every other corner. Maui continues to attract fine chefs, some of whom have initiated the trend La Bretagne owner/chef Claude Gaty calls "nouvelle Hawaiian." This growing movement uses fruits and vegetables unique to Hawaii in classic European or Asian ways—spawning such dishes as breadfruit soufflé and papaya cheesecake. Sometimes a touch of California is added as well.

Of course, you can find plain old local-style cooking on the Valley Isle—particularly if you wander into the less touristy areas of Wailuku or Kahului, for example. Greasy spoons abound, and some of those places are where you can get the most authentic local food, or what residents call "plate lunch," for very little expense. A good plate lunch will fulfill your daily requirement of carbohydrates: macaroni salad, two scoops of rice, and an entrée of, say, curry stew, teriyaki beef, or *kalua* (roasted) pig and cabbage.

Some of the island's best restaurants are in hotels—not surprising, considering that tourism is the island's number one industry. In the resorts, you'll find some of Maui's finest Continental restaurants, and some good coffee shops as well. In addition, because many of the upscale hotels sit right on the beach, you'll often have the benefit of an oceanfront ambience. Few restaurants on Maui require jackets. An aloha shirt and pants for men, and a simple dress or pants for women are acceptable in all but the fanciest establishments.

Restaurants are open daily unless otherwise noted.

Highly recommended restaurants in each price category are indicated by a star ★.

Category	Cost*
Very Expensive	over $60
Expensive	$40–$60
Moderate	$20–$40
Inexpensive	under $20

*per person, excluding drinks, service, and sales tax (4%)

West Maui

American   **Lahaina Provision Co.** This small place, located in the Hyatt Regency, serves a tasty lunch buffet, as well as sandwiches, steak, and seafood; there's also a well-stocked salad bar. At 6 PM, it opens its Chocoholic Bar, and until 10:30, you can get chocolate treats of every variety: brownies, double-fudge cake, white-chocolate mousse, chocolate-chip cookies, chocolate candies, and ice cream with hot fudge, bittersweet chocolate, or white chocolate-coconut sauce. If you like chocolate, this is the place. *Hyatt Regency Maui, 200 Nohea Kai Dr., Kaanapali, tel. 808/661–1234. Dress: casual. AE, DC, MC, V. Moderate.*
Leilani's on the Beach. This little spot is a local success story. Its owners also operate Kimo's in Lahaina and the Grill & Bar at Kapalua. You'll dine in a relaxing, contemporary atmosphere

Alex's Hole in the Wall, **10**

Avalon Restaurant and Bar, **9**

The Bay Club, **1**

Bullock's, **32**

Casanova Italian Restaurant & Deli, **30**

The Chart House, **22**

Chez Paul, **17**

Chopsticks, **4**

Dillon's, **26**

Erik's Seafood Grotto, **3**

Gerard's, **12**

Haliimaile General Store, **28**

Ichiban, **23**

Island Fish House, **34**

La Bretagne, **15**

La Perouse, **36**

Lahaina Coolers, **13**

Lahaina Provision Co., **7**

Leilani's on the Beach, **5**

Longhi's, **8**

Makawao Steak House, **29**

Mama's Fish House, **25**

Mark Edison's, **18**

Maui Onion, **35**

Ming Yuen, **24**

Moon Hoe Seafood Restaurant, **19**

Nikko, **6**

Orient Express, **2**

Palm Court, **35**

Picnics, **27**

Pineapple Hill, **1**

Plantation Veranda, **1**

Polli's, **31, 33**

Prince Court, **37**

Raffles, **35**

Saeng's Thai Cuisine, **21**

Sam's Upstairs, **16**

Scaroles Italian Ristorante and Pizzeria, **11**

Siam Thai, **20**

Swan Court, **7**

Tasca, **14**

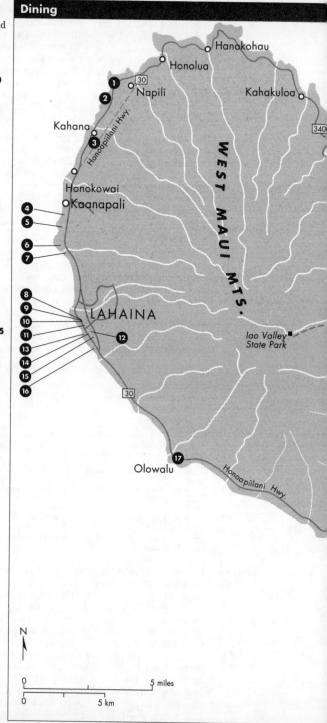

Dining

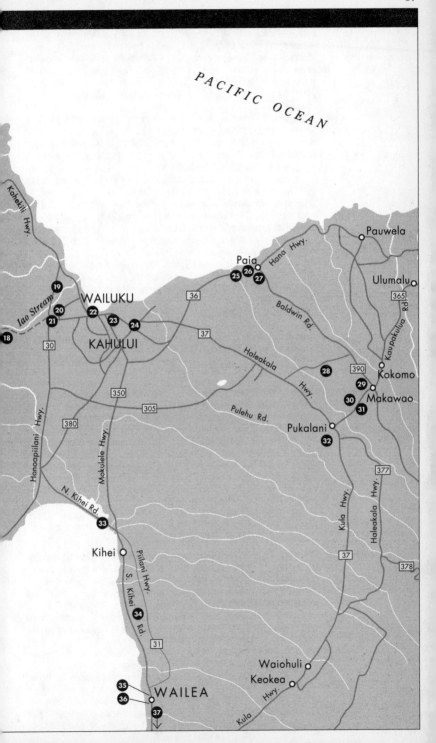

PACIFIC OCEAN

Kahekili Hwy.

Iao Stream

19

WAILUKU

20

21

22

23

24

18

30

KAHULUI

36

Pauwela

Paia

25 26

27

Hana Hwy.

Ulumalu

365

Baldwin Rd.

37

Haleakala

28

390

Kaupakulua Rd.

Kokomo

29

Makawao

350

Hwy.

30

305

Pulehu Rd.

31

380

Honoapiilani Hwy.

Mokulele Hwy.

Pukalani

32

377

N. Kihei Rd

33

Kihei

Piilani Hwy.

S. Kihei Rd.

Kula Hwy.

Haleakala Hwy.

37

378

34

31

Waiohuli

Keokea

35

36

WAILEA

37

Kula Hwy.

with a good view of the Kaanapali Resort. Dinner each evening includes such specialties as baby back ribs, smoked daily; three or four varieties of fresh fish; and steak and lobster. A downstairs seafood bar opens at 4 PM, with smaller portions and lower prices (between $4.95 and $9.95). *Whalers Village, 2435 Kaanapali Pkwy., Kaanapali Beach Resort, tel. 808/661–4495. Reservations advised. Dress: casual. AE, MC, V. Moderate.*

★ **Longhi's.** Proprietor Bob Longhi has gotten a lot of notoriety for the way his young waiters and waitresses pull up a chair and recite the day's menu. But what makes this establishment worth a visit is the food. Homemade pasta and pastry—whipped up by the full-time pastry chef—as well as fresh-squeezed orange juice, fresh fish, and sandwiches you can't get your mouth around are only some of the choices here. Longhi's is an open-air establishment on its first floor; tile floors and casual wood tables invite celebrities, as well as more run-of-the-mill diners, to stop and watch the world go by while supping on an enormous burger, French onion soup made with Maui onions, or a lobster caught in waters right offshore. This is a good choice for breakfast and opens at 7:30. At night, the upper floor offers a fancier version of dinner, with dancing. *888 Front St., Lahaina, tel. 808/667–2288. No reservations. Dress: casual. AE, V. Moderate.*

Sam's Upstairs. This open-air bistro in a relatively uncrowded section of Lahaina gives good views of the ocean and Lanai beyond. Dinners feature tender steaks, fresh local fish, and Maine lobster. The more casual Sam's Pub downstairs serves lunch. *505 Front St., Lahaina, tel. 808/667–4341. Reservations advised. Dress: casual. AE, MC, V. Moderate–Expensive.*

Chinese Chopsticks. When it opened a few years back, this was Maui's first restaurant featuring "grazing"—the sampling of several appetizer-size portions in lieu of a single entrée. Here, you'll find yourself enjoying the cuisines of China, Japan, Thailand, and Polynesia. A typical meal might include the likes of Chinese dim sum (wonton-wrapped bits of meat and fish), Japanese sushi, and Thai spring rolls (like egg rolls only crisper and served with mint leaves, cucumber, and lettuce). The atmosphere is friendly, but keep an eye on your tab—watch what seems to be an inexpensive meal add up with each morsel you select. *Royal Lahaina Hotel, Kaanapali Beach Resort, 2780 Kekaa Dr., tel. 808/661–3611. No reservations. Dress: casual. AE, DC, MC, V. Inexpensive–Moderate.*

Continental The Bay Club. Here's just the place to have a magical candle-
★ light dinner. This restaurant is situated on a lava-rock promontory overlooking the bay at the far end of Kapalua Beach, within the Kapalua Resort. Set in an open-air room, with richly paneled walls and rattan furniture, the Bay Club has an excellent wine list and nouvelle cuisine menu; the scaloppine of veal and fresh catch of the day from the Molokai Channel are both superior choices. *At the Kapalua Bay Resort, 1 Bay Dr., Kapalua, tel. 808/669–5656. Reservations required. Jacket required at dinner. AE, DC, MC, V. Expensive.*

★ **Plantation Veranda.** Raffles fans stirring a gentle breeze above, hand-polished mahogany floors with hooked rugs, and Windsor chairs make this place reminiscent of an old Hawaiian plantation house. The menu is extensive: from saffron-poached fish of the day to escallops of spring lamb to chateaubriand for two.

Try the homemade pâté, which is excellent, then move on to, perhaps, the galantine of young island duck or the paillard of veal with scampi and bay scallops. *Kapalua Bay Hotel, 1 Bay Dr., Kapalua, tel. 808/669–5656. Reservations required. Jacket required. AE, DC, MC, V. Expensive.*

Swan Court. You enter by descending a grand staircase to the edge of a lagoon in which swans glide by. A waterfall splashes, and palm fronds sway slightly in the breeze—the Swan Court radiates grandeur and elegance. The international menu includes fresh island fish Eichenholz, which is baked on an oak plate with capers and mushroom garnish; roasted baby chicken in a sour-mash bourbon sauce; veal chop sauté Armagnac, in cream with sorrel mushrooms; and roast duck, chateaubriand, fresh fish, and more. The Swan Court's extensive wine list has won awards of excellence from *Wine Spectator* magazine. The restaurant is open for a breakfast buffet. *Hyatt Regency Maui, Kaanapali Beach Resort, 200 Nohea Kai Dr., tel. 808/661–1234. Reservations advised. Jacket required. AE, DC, MC, V. Expensive.*

Pineapple Hill. The newest establishment at the Kapalua Resort is located in an old plantation home built in 1915 for D. T. Fleming, one of the Hawaiian pineapple industry's founding fathers. The home is set high above the Pacific at the end of a drive flanked by towering Norfolk pines and boasts a large rock fireplace and a delightful waterfall off the patio. You can choose from such appetizers as stuffed mushrooms, fresh oysters, and French onion soup; entrées may include chicken with a guava glaze in a pineapple boat, king scallops au gratin, and Hawaiian teriyaki steak, as well as buckets of fresh steamer clams, prime rib, lamb, duck, and lobster. *Kapalua Resort, 1000 Kapalua Dr., tel. 808/669–6129. Reservations advised. Dress: casual. AE, DC, MC, V. Dinner only. Moderate–Expensive.*

French ★ **Chez Paul.** A mere wide spot in the road, 4 miles south of Lahaina in Olowalu, provides the setting for this intimate French restaurant that's made a name for itself since 1975. Chez Paul has only 14 tables, each set with linen tablecloths, china, and fresh flowers. The menu changes daily, but specialties include scampi Olowalu, cooked with white wine, herbs, and capers; poisson beurre blanc, fresh island fish poached in white wine with shallots, cream, and capers; and veal à la Normande, sautéed with green apples in a Calvados sauce. If you're still hungry, try the Kahlua cheesecake. *On Hwy. 30, 4 mi south of Lahaina, tel. 808/661–3843. Reservations required. Dress: casual chic. AE, MC, V. 2 dinner seatings nightly, at 6:30 and 8:30. Expensive.*

★ **La Bretagne.** Chef/owner Claude Gaty wasn't raised in the kitchen, but the native Frenchman turns out some of the tastiest cuisine this side of Paris. Such dishes as seafood à la Bretonne (in puff pastry), duck with pear à la Williams, beef tournedos, and rack of lamb waltz out of Gaty's galley each night to satisfy the eager diners who pack the little restaurant. La Bretagne is set in a house the town sheriff built in 1920. It's now a little run-down but still reminiscent of a French country inn. Soft brocade wallpaper and flowered draperies decorate the inside, while a screened-in porch provides a more open-air ambience. Right inside the door, a gleaming brass espresso machine gives La Bretagne that nonchalant European touch. The lighting is low, the service is friendly, the food is fantastic. What else is there? *562-C Front St., facing Maluulu o lele*

Park, Lahaina, tel. 808/661–8966. Reservations advised.
Dress: casual. AE, MC, V. Expensive.

★ **Gerard's.** Set in the romantic, Victorian-style Plantation Inn,
this restaurant is the creation of owner Gerard Reversade, one
of Hawaii's most talented chefs. Gerard's serves French cuisine, with a menu that changes daily. Two recommended dishes
are rack of lamb and medallions of veal duxelles with ravioli.
Other specialties include fresh fish, lamb, beef, veal, and 75
wine varieties. This place has a comfortable ambience, great
food, and plenty of stargazing possibilities—it's a celebrity favorite. At the Plantation Inn, 174 Lahainaluna Rd., Lahaina,
tel. 808/661–8939. Reservations required. Dress: casual. AE,
DC, MC, V. Dinner only. Expensive.

Italian **Alex's Hole in the Wall.** When Alex and Tom Didio came to Ha-
★ waii more than 30 years ago, they brought their grandpa
Marchetti's family recipes, determined to put them to good use
someday. In 1971, Alex's Hole in the Wall started making
Grandpa proud. Look for the restaurant down a narrow alley
behind the Dolphin Gallery and up a staircase. Inside, you'll
think you're in an Italian living room, since the place is
crammed with knickknacks of all kinds. The brothers make
their own pasta and sausage; favorite dishes include *pollo
e'salsicca* (chicken with garlic and sausage) and lasagne
imbottita (with spinach, meat, and four cheeses). The desserts
are to die for—try the cheesecake with rum and tropical fruit.
834 Front St., Lahaina, tel. 808/661–3197. No reservations.
Dress: casual. AE, MC, V. Inexpensive–Moderate.

Scaroles Italian Ristorante and Pizzeria. Step into the ambience
of the old country as dinner at Scaroles puts you in the midst of
Italian art deco. Try the New York–style thin-crust pizza or
the mozarella marinara, and finish off with ricotta cheesecake.
If you prefer, Scaroles will deliver any dish to your West Maui
hotel or condo. 930 Wainee St., Lahaina, tel. 808/661–4466.
Reservations advised. Dress: casual. MC, V. Moderate.

Japanese **Nikko.** This is Japanese food *teppan* style. That means you'll be
seated with other diners at a table that has a built-in grill. Together you'll watch the chef and his slicing, dicing, and chop-
ping knives. He can perform amazing feats—and the best part
is you get to eat the creations he prepares. Vegetables, such as
green peppers, eggplant, and squash, as well as bite-size chick-
en, pork, and beef, are grilled to perfection. A lot of Japanese
visitors find their way to Nikko—and you know what that says
about a place. Maui Marriott Hotel, Kaanapali Beach Resort,
100 Nohea Kai Dr., tel. 808/667–1200. Reservations required.
Dress: casual. AE, DC, MC, V. Moderate.

Seafood **Erik's Seafood Grotto.** This award-winning restaurant and oys-
ter bar in the Kahana Villas Condominiums offers a netful of
fresh island fish daily, plus such flavorful house specialties as
cioppino and seafood curry. The fresh Hawaiian spiny or slip-
per lobster is filled with seafood stuffing and flame-broiled,
while you can get your *opakapaka* (blue snapper) sautéed with
butter. The mahimahi is especially delicious baked in vermouth
with macadamia nuts. If you arrive between 5 and 6 PM you can
sample the $10.95 early-bird special. Erik's also offers *keiki*
dinners—a petite steak or medley of chicken, fish, and shrimp
at $8.95 for children under 12. Erik's has a nautical feel to it,
with a rustic open-beam ceiling and lots of hanging plants.
Kahana Villas, 4242 Lower Honoapiilani Hwy., Kahana, tel.

808/669–4806. Reservations advised. Dress: casual. AE, MC, V. Dinner only. Moderate.

Spanish **Tasca.** This restaurant specializes in "tapas," the Spanish equivalent of "pupus" in Hawaii or "hors d'oeuvres" in America. The Mediterranean-style paella, ceviche, ratatouille, and other tasty nuggets hail from countries such as Greece, Portugal, Italy—and even Spain. *608 Front St., Lahaina, tel. 808/ 661–8001. Reservations not necessary. Dress: casual. AE, MC, V. Inexpensive–Moderate.*

Thai **Orient Express.** Red lacquer carvings are contrasted here with splashes of yellow flowers and a decorative fountain to create an airy Asian atmosphere. The house specialties include the delicious Szechuan Kung Pao shrimp, cooked with dried chiles, bamboo shoots, and water chestnuts; coconut chicken soup, consisting of coconut milk, *kiffir* leaves, and mushrooms; and sate, made with beef strips marinated in spices and coconut milk, then speared on bamboo sticks and grilled. As at most Thai restaurants, dishes here can be ordered hot, medium, or mild. Between 5:30 PM and 7 PM, the five-course early-bird special goes for $9.95. *Napili Shores Resort, 5316 Lower Honoapiilani Hwy., Napili, tel. 808/669–8077. Reservations advised. Dress: casual. AE, MC, V. Dinner only. Moderate.*

Tropical/ Continental ★ **Avalon Restaurant and Bar.** This is one of Maui's newest and trendiest restaurants. Mark Ellman is a young Californian who came to Maui and opened his first commercial venture in January 1988, with Ellman in the kitchen. The decor at the Avalon is Hawaiian 1940s, with bright tropical prints on the chairs and tables, reminiscent of the days when you had to cruise to the Islands and, once there, would find a paradise of swaying palms and hula girls. Oversize dishware brings the food to the table— and what food it is! The owner calls it "Pacific Rim," and it features cuisine from California, Hawaii, Mexico, Indonesia, Thailand, Vietnam, and Japan. Ellman's signature items include roast duck with plum sauce and Chinese steamed dumplings; giant prawns in a garlic black-bean sauce; and fresh guacamole made right at your table. For dessert, try the pineapple upside-down cake served warm with whipped cream or the caramel Miranda—fresh exotic fruits in a homemade caramel sauce with sour cream and brown sugar. Celebrities love the Avalon: During one four-day visit, Yoko Ono was seen there three nights. *Mariner's Alley, 844 Front St., Lahaina, tel. 808/667– 5559. Reservations advised. Dress: casual. AE, DC, MC, V. Moderate.*

★ **Lahaina Coolers.** This surf bistro specializes in unusual food at reasonable prices. Try the pepper chicken linguini in a sauce of roasted bell peppers, or a spinach and feta quesadilla. *180 Dickenson St., Lahaina, tel. 808/661–7082. Reservations advised. Dress: casual. AE, MC, V. Inexpensive.*

Central Maui

American **Mark Edison's.** A romantic dining spot, Mark Edison's boasts one of Maui's most unusual locations. With views of the West Maui mountains and Iao Valley Park, this restaurant has a lush, tropical ambience unlike that of any other eating establishment. Specialties include chicken, steak, pasta, and fish, with a well-stocked salad bar. Each day from 5:30 to 6:30, you can order prime rib and teriyaki chicken at $8.95. Mark Edison's has a large local following, especially at lunch. It also brings in good entertainment at least once a week. *Iao Valley Rd., just beyond Kepaniwai Park at the Iao Needle, tel. 808/242–5555. Reservations advised. Dress: casual. AE, MC, V. Moderate–Expensive.*

Chinese **Ming Yuen.** This place is low-key, with unassuming decor, but
★ locals love it and will line up to prove it. The menu is extensive and features mostly Cantonese cuisine, plus a few Szechuan dishes. The lemon chicken has made it famous, but you might try the hot-and-sour soup to start and then go for the Kung Pao chicken: chicken stir-fried with chili peppers, garlic, peanuts, and chopped vegetables. The mu-shu pork is also recommended. Ming Yuen's most unusual dish is a minced squab cooked in a Chinese mushroom sauce and served in lettuce pockets. *162 Alamaha St., Kahului, tel. 808/871–7787. Reservations advised. Dress: casual. AE, DC, MC, V. Inexpensive.*

Moon Hoe Seafood Restaurant. The second really good Chinese restaurant on Maui, Moon Hoe offers both Cantonese and Szechuan cuisines, with more than 100 different dishes to choose from, including a popular crispy roast chicken and a beef with snow peas. The fresh island-caught fish is superb. *752 Lower Main St., Wailuku, tel. 808/242–7778. Reservations advised. Dress: casual. MC, V. Inexpensive.*

Japanese **Ichiban.** If you've a hankering to try Japanese food in Maui, this is the place to do it. There's nothing fancy here, but you'll find authentic sashimi, teriyaki, and noodle dishes. The shrimp tempura and the combination dish are both popular and recommended. *Kahului Shopping Center, 2133 Kaohu St., Kahului, tel. 808/871–6977. Dress: casual. MC, V. Inexpensive.*

Steakhouse **The Chart House.** This dining spot is about as close to the ocean as you can get in a Kahului restaurant. Large aquariums that serve as partial walls contribute to the nautical decor. The menu includes steaks grilled to order; fresh fish sautéed, baked, broiled, or cooked in herbs and spices; and a well-stocked salad bar. One of the nicest dining establishments for both food and ambience in Kahului, the Chart House is very popular with the local after-work crowd. *500 Puunene Ave., Kahului, tel. 808/877–2476. Reservations advised. Dress: casual. AE, MC, V. Moderate.*

Thai **Saeng's Thai Cuisine.** This hot spot has received quite a bit of attention since it first opened in 1989. Specialties include Evil Prince chicken (cooked in coconut sauce with Thai herbs) and Kai-Yang (grilled chicken seasoned with lemongrass and Thai special sauce). The spicy vegetarian dishes are also delicious. Exotic flowers and a waterfall view enhance the tropical decor. *2119 Vineyard, Wailuku, tel. 808/244–1567. Reservations advised. Dress: casual. MC, V. No lunch weekends. Inexpensive–Moderate.*

Siam Thai. This is one of the best places to sample Thai cuisine in the Islands—and such celebrities as Robert Redford (whose picture adorns the wall) will probably vouch for it. There are about 70 selections on the menu, including some fine vegetarian dishes. The specialties are the curries, which come in red, green, or yellow, and hot, medium, or mild. Plants grace the interior, while white tablecloths add a touch of class. *123 Market, Wailuku, tel. 808/244–3817. Reservations advised. Dress: casual. AE, MC, V. Inexpensive–Moderate.*

East Maui

American **Bullock's.** It isn't easy to get a good burger on Maui, but the large Moonburgers here are terrific, so it's easy to see what attracts the locals. The shakes are recommended, too, particularly the ones featuring such tropical fruits as guava and papaya. A lot of people stop here on their way to or from Haleakala, because it's located in Pukalani, about 10 miles up the Haleakala Highway. *3494 Haleakala Hwy., Pukalani, tel. 808/572–7220. Dress: casual. MC, V. Closed for dinner. Inexpensive.*

Maui Onion. Set out by the pool at the Stouffer Wailea Hotel, this coffee shop has a small menu that includes salads and sandwiches. Maui Onion made it onto this list, however, because of its mouth-watering Maui onion rings. If you love onion rings, we recommend you make a special trip here. *Stouffer Wailea Hotel, Wailea Resort, 3550 Wailea Alanui Dr., tel. 808/879–4900. Dress: casual. AE, DC, MC, V. Inexpensive.*

Buffet **Palm Court.** This is another Stouffer restaurant with a twist: At the Palm Court, you will find a huge buffet each night. What's more, the Palm Court rotates cuisines so that one night it will serve pasta, the next a paniolo steak fry, and two nights each week feature seafood or English cuisine. Those who'd rather not partake of the buffet can order from the menu. *Stouffer Wailea Beach Resort, 3550 Wailea Alanui Dr., tel. 808/879–4900. Reservations advised. Dress: casual. AE, DC, MC, V. Moderate.*

Continental **La Perouse.** This hushed, intimate room, richly paneled in koa ★ and decorated with antiques and objets d'art, is named after the French explorer who discovered Maui in 1786. La Perouse serves as a worthy competitor to Raffles next door. Although the menu changes monthly, the accent here is on delicacies native to Hawaii—the island snapper with wild Haiku mushrooms is excellent, as is the creamy callaloo of crab meat soup with Maui taro leaves, the deep-water abalone with creamy dill sauce, and the beef tenderloin filled with pepper cheeses. The emphasis here is on seafood, but you can also get duck, lamb, chicken, or beef. Polish off your meal with the decadent chocolate mousse Brasilia. *Maui Inter-Continental Wailea Hotel, Wailea, tel. 808/879–1922. Reservations required. Dress: casual. AE, DC, MC, V. Very Expensive.*

★ **Raffles.** The pride and joy of the Stouffer Wailea Beach Resort, Raffles is a luxurious, award-winning room that pays homage to British colonial elegance. In fact, the name was inspired by Sir Thomas Stamford Raffles (1781–1826), founder of the city of Singapore; the Raffles Hotel in that city is world renowned. In this restaurant, Oriental rugs rest on shining teak floors, and bronze chandeliers illuminate the Chinese ceramics. The sophisticated Continental cuisine includes such treats as opakapaka with avocado mango cream; ono in burgundy with papaya and tomato coulis; and grilled ahi steak with eggplant, wasabe, ginger, cream, and green tea noodles. The Singapore Sling sorbet served between courses is a nice touch. Raffles also has an extravagant Sunday brunch that features, among other things, omelets and strawberries dipped in chocolate. *Stouffer Wailea Beach Resort, 3550 Wailea Alanui Dr., tel. 808/879–4900. Reservations required. Dress: casual but chic. AE, DC, MC, V. Very Expensive.*

★ **Prince Court.** This fine-dining restaurant, located in the Maui Prince Hotel, has made a name for itself with the help of its innovative chef, Roger Dikon. Although it bills itself as an American restaurant, it seems to belong in the Continental category, with the other classy establishments. The view of the ocean is marvelous at this romantic place which offers exquisite candlelit dining on two levels, and excellent service in a long room decorated with bamboo-cushioned chairs, island plants, and tropical flowers. The chef puts together a delectable prix-fixe menu, usually featuring fish specialties and luscious desserts, such as Strawberry Bombe in Chocolate. Although the chef's creativity with the island's fresh seafood is most notable, you'll also find dependable continental fare such as veal, rack of lamb, and local fish, complemented by an extensive wine list. The restaurant also features a wonderful Sunday brunch from 10 to 2. *Maui Prince Hotel, Makena Resort, Makena, tel. 808/ 874–1111. Reservations advised. Jacket advised at dinner. AE, DC, MC, V. Dinner and Sun. brunch only. Expensive.*

Italian **Casanova Italian Restaurant & Deli.** Owned by three young native Italians—and a German brought up in Italy—this Upcountry establishment has expanded into a real restaurant offering the best Italian food on Maui. A wood-fired pizza oven produces a variety of yummy pies; try the salsiccia with mozzarella, ham, and broccoli in a tomato sauce. You can also order pasta, chicken, or fresh fish. *1188 Makawao Ave., Makawao, tel. 808/572–0220. Reservations advised. Dress: casual. AE, MC, V. Moderate.*

Mexican **Polli's.** ★ Who would've thought you could find two vegetarian Mexican restaurants on Maui? Native Arizonan Polli Smith and her husband started La Familia several years ago, sold it, then opened a lively Mexican cantina called Polli's in Upcountry Makawao. It was so successful, they opened Polli's on the Beach in Kihei, which features an open-air atmosphere perfect for Maui sunsets. They've now added meat to the menu, but their meatless tacos, burritos, and enchiladas are just as good. Everything's offered à la carte, but you can get complete dinners, too. Polli's margaritas are the best in the state—take it from us. *1202 Makawao Ave., Makawao, tel. 808/572–7808, and 101 N. Kihei Rd., Kihei, tel. 808/879–5275. Reservations advised. Dress: casual. AE, MC, V. Inexpensive.*

Seafood **Island Fish House.** At this relaxed and reliable seafood spot, four or five fresh catches are usually available—mahimahi, ono, ahi, onaga, and opakapaka. You have a choice of preparations—baked, broiled, deep-fried, poached, sautéed, teriyaki style, or even in a champagne sauce. The Chef's Trio provides a selection of three kinds of fish; you can also sample from one of Maui's most impressive lists of California chardonnays. *1945 S. Kihei Rd., Kihei, tel. 808/879–7771. Reservations advised. Dress: casual. AE, MC, V. Moderate.*

★ **Mama's Fish House.** Looking for the best seafood on Maui? Put your car on the Hana Highway and head toward Paia. About 1½ miles before Paia, you'll see an oceanfront building on your left—Mama's, an Old Hawaiian–style restaurant serving honest food. This is a lovely spot, well landscaped and well tended. The fresh fish here has the reputation of being the best you can find in the area, and you can get it sautéed in butter, poached in white wine sauce with mushrooms, or broiled with lemon butter. One recommended dish is the stuffed fish Lani, a fresh fish fillet baked with Mama's shrimp stuffing. Mama's also serves meat and chicken. *799 Kaiholo Pl., Paia, tel. 808/579–9672.*

Reservations required at dinner. Dress: casual. AE, MC, V. Moderate.

Steakhouse **Makawao Steak House.** This popular Upcountry dinner house is arguably one of the best steak joints on the island—a tender top sirloin goes for less than $25. The fresh fish, salad bar, and fresh-baked bread are just as good. If you really decide to splurge, you can get scampi and lobster. But meat lovers shouldn't miss the steak. *3612 Baldwin Ave., tel. 808/572–8711. Dress: casual. AE, MC, V. Dinner only, with specials offered before 6. Moderate.*

Tropical/ **Haliimaile General Store.** This delightful restaurant was a
Continental camp store in the 1920s, but you'd never know it now. From the
★ outside, its white, green, and peach tin exterior looks a little out of place, sitting proudly in a pineapple field in Upcountry Maui, literally in the middle of nowhere. Owner Beverly Gannon has done wonders with this place, turning it into a charming outpost that serves some of the best food in the state. The contemporary menu uses Island products which change with the seasons. One of Haliimaile's staples is duck prepared in a variety of ways, such as duck smoked with pineapple chutney. Other specialties include the dynamite barbecued ribs, lobster pasta with fresh tarragon, and spicy shrimp Diane. Mrs. Gannon intended to open a deli with only 32 seats—although it grew to 80 within one week—and there's a stainless steel deli case featuring all the different specials. A corner of this restaurant looks like an old general store, with items for sale. Since its opening in 1988, this has become one of Maui's most magnetic restaurants, repeatedly attracting celebrities and a host of other see-and-be-seen types. *Haliimaile Rd., 2 mi before Pukalani, tel. 808/572–2666. Dress: casual. AE, MC, V. Closed Mon. Moderate–Expensive.*

Picnics

On Maui, you'll find plenty of places with a secluded spot for a lap-top lunch for two. Also, if you're on your way to Haleakala or Hana, you might want to take along a picnic. A few companies put together meals that will make your outing more satisfying. Prices vary depending on what you order. Be sure to call ahead. Here's one recommendation:

Picnics. This shop specializes in picnics for Hana trips. Its large menu (with a map of Maui on the back) includes fresh Maui fruits, veggies, a variety of other items, such as burgers, roast beef, turkey, kiawe-broiled chicken, nut bread, and cookies. *30 Baldwin Ave., Paia, tel. 808/579–8021. No credit cards.*

If you want to put together your own picnic, try one of these Maui delis:

Casanova Italian Restaurant & Deli (1188 Makawao Ave., Makawao, tel. 808/572–0220).
Goodies Etc. & Co. (888 Front St., Lahaina, tel. 808/661–0943).
The New York Deli (2395 S. Kihei Rd., Kihei, tel. 808/879–1115).
Ricco's Old World Delicatessen (Whalers Village, 2435 Kaanapali Pkwy., Kaanapali, tel. 808/661–4433).

7 Lodging

Maui has the state's highest concentration of condominium units. More than half of the island's rental units, in fact, are condos. Don't be put off by this; it's not what you're thinking. For the most part, Maui's condos are not the tacky high rises that boast thin walls and cheap appliances. These are top-of-the-line units with all the amenities. Many are oceanfront and offer the ambience of a hotel suite without the cost.

Maui also boasts the highest percentage of luxury hotel rooms in the state. According to a national hotel-research firm, a full 50% of the Valley Isle's hotel rooms can be placed in the stratosphere when it comes to elegance. And although the figure for luxury condominiums is lower, you can nonetheless find some outrageously upscale condos on the Valley Isle.

Of course, the price you'll pay to stay on Maui reflects this attention to luxury. The island has the highest average accommodation cost of any Hawaiian island, and hoteliers here have tended in the past to raise rates with much greater abandon. In recent years, this has created a greater willingness on the part of visitors to try other islands, which is one reason Kauai and the Big Island have had higher visitor counts and occupancy rates. The average lodging rate on Maui can run as much as $70 more a night than on the other islands. Most lodgings come equipped with swimming pools, all of them outdoors to take full advantage of the gentle year-round climate.

What you'll pay depends in part on where you want to stay. West Maui is the center of tourism. More rooms are available on this part of the Valley Island than anywhere else, and most are high quality, and expensive. Two major resort areas anchor West Maui: the Kaanapali Beach Resort, with its six hotels and seven condominiums, and the Kapalua Bay Resort, with its one hotel and one condo.

Central Maui is a tough place to stay, mostly because the choices are so limited. It's a small area to begin with, and Central Maui is better known as home to the majority of the Valley Isle's residents. Wailuku is the county seat, and Kahului is the industrial/commercial center; neither place offers much in the way of accommodations. Kahului has two hotels that are decent; Maalaea harbor has a few passable condos. Then there are the hangouts, flophouses, and the like for the windsurfers who seem to have found a permanent home on Maui. Unless you're one of them, you probably won't enjoy these rooms.

East Maui is a mixed bag when it comes to accommodations. You can find just about any rate and just about any degree of comfort. That's partly because the area is so huge, encompassing:

1) the Wailea and Makena resorts along the southwestern shore, which are both master-planned, full-service accommodations with fairly steep prices to match;

2) Kihei, a hodgepodge strip running north from Wailea, dotted mostly with condo units that have a range of amenities and fairly reasonable prices;

3) Upcountry Maui, the area that rises into the clouds of Haleakala, with a couple of lodges, but mostly bed-and-breakfasts, if anything;

4) Hana, secluded in the easternmost part of Maui, with only a few lodgings, whose prices range from inexpensive to very expensive.

Except during the peak months of February and August, you should have no trouble getting a room on Maui. When making your reservations, either on your own or through a travel agent, ask about packages and extras. Some hotels have special tennis, golf, or honeymoon packages. Others have periodic room-and-car packages. All of the above will cut your per-night cost.

Highly recommended hotels in each price category are indicated by a star ★ .

Category	Cost*
Very Expensive	over $175
Expensive	$125–$175
Moderate	$75–$125
Inexpensive	under $75

All prices are for a standard double room, excluding 9¼% tax and service charges.

West Maui

Very Expensive   **Embassy Suites.** The Hawaiian Islands' first all-suite hotel opened north of Kaanapali in late 1988 with one- and two-bedroom apartments. The units are spacious, with a blue-and-beige decor that gently insists on being trendily tropical. Each suite has two phones (with separate phone lines), ceiling fans, air-conditioning, a refrigerator, a microwave oven, and a coffee maker, as well as a 36-inch color television with a VCR. Fine touches have been added, such as an inviting wicker chaise longue perched next to an open window. The rates include a full breakfast each morning and a two-hour cocktail party with manager Gary Ettinger each evening. *104 Kaanapali Shores Pl., Lahaina 96761, tel. 808/661–2000 or 800/462–6284. 413 units. Beachfront. Facilities: sauna, health club, pool, tennis, golf, A/C, color TV. AE, DC, MC, V.*

Hyatt Regency Maui. Want to stay in a fantasyland? This lavish property was built in 1980 by Chris Hemmeter, a developer with a penchant for water fantasies and expensive art, and the hotel shows his biases. There are nine major waterfalls and several smaller ones. The 750,000-gallon pool is something every honeymooning couple should have access to—there's a secret, romantic grotto made more secluded by a waterfall cascading over the opening, as well as a 130-foot water slide, a swinging rope bridge, and a swim-up cocktail bar. A $12 million renovation has made the rooms better than ever. *200 Nohea Kai Dr., Lahaina 96761, tel. 808/661–1234 or 800/233–1234. 815 rooms with bath. Beachfront. Facilities: 5 restaurants, 7 cocktail lounges, golf, tennis, color TV, A/C, library, health spa. AE, DC, MC, V.*

Kaanapali Alii. This is a condominium, but you'd never know it; the four 11-story buildings are put together so well, you still have the feeling of seclusion. Instead of tiny rooms, you can choose from one- and two-bedroom apartments. Each features lovely amenities: a chaise in an alcove, a bidet, a sunken living room, a whirlpool, oak kitchen cabinets, and a separate dining room. Run by a company called Classic Resorts, the Kaanapali Alii is maintained like a hotel—with daily maid service, an Activities Desk, and a 24-hour front desk. If you can afford the nightly rate, it's well worth the price. *50 Nohea Kai Dr., Lahaina 96761, tel. 808/667–1400 or 800/642–MAUI. 264 1- and 2-bedroom units with bath. Beachfront. Facilities: sauna, pools, lighted tennis courts, golf, A/C, color TV. AE, DC, MC, V.*

★ **Kapalua Bay Hotel.** Part of the Kapalua Bay Resort, this is one of the finest hotels in the state, winner of numerous awards and accolades. Built in 1978, the hotel has a California feel to it: the exterior is all understated white and natural wood. The open lobby, filled with flowering vanda and dendrobium orchids, has a fine view of the ocean beyond. The rooms are spacious and have recently been renovated. The impeccable staff is always ready to fill any need, and for the price, you certainly won't be disappointed. Although it's isolated from other resort areas, Kapalua has some of the island's finest restaurants and shops to make up for it. *1 Bay Dr., Kapalua 96761, tel. 808/669–5656 or 800/367–8000. 194 rooms with bath. (There are also 135 1- and 2-bedroom units in the Kapalua Villas on the Kapalua Resort. Condo rates are higher than hotel prices and often include a car.) Beachfront. Facilities: pool, 4 restaurants, shops, color TV, A/C, golf, and tennis. AE, DC, MC, V.*

★ **Maui Marriott.** The Marriott sits on the same impressive Kaanapali beach as the Hyatt and Westin, but its rooms and service offer a lot less flash. The rooms are large—90% have ocean views—decorated in shades of mauve and mint with floral-pattern drapes and bamboo furniture, while the lobby is open and airy and filled with cascading orchids. The best thing about the Marriott, however, is the service. Most hotels talk about a guest-oriented staff; the Marriott lives the notion. These people are genuinely friendly and helpful. You almost think they'll invite you home for a visit. Maui's best Japanese restaurant, Nikko, is on the ground floor. The Lokelani specializes in fish entrées, while the cheerful Mauna Terrace features open-air dining and more casual fare. *100 Nohea Kai Dr., Lahaina 96761, tel. 808/667–1200 or 800/228–9290. 720 rooms with bath. Beachfront. Facilities: 4 restaurants, 3 lounges, tennis, disco, color TV, golf, pool. AC, DC, MC, V.*

Puunoa Beach Estates. Economically speaking, this place is in another universe: Prices for a two-bedroom start at about $550. But you may be looking for the kind of pampering you'll get here. With only 8 units in the secluded beachfront property, set between Kaanapali and Lahaina, guests can expect iced champagne upon arrival, terry-cloth robes, fully stocked in-room bars, outdoor Jacuzzis, daily in-room copies of the *Wall Street Journal*, and a concierge ready to help plan their stay. Rooms are tastefully furnished, with such homey touches as koa-wood bookcases, floral bedspreads, and skylights. *45 Kai Pali Pl., Lahaina 96761, tel. 808/667–5972 or 800/642–MAUI. 8 units with bath, on the beach. Facilities: sauna, pool, Jacuzzi, tennis, concierge, daily maid service. Some rates include a car. AE, MC, V.*

Sheraton Maui. One of Kaanapali's oldest hotels, the Sheraton opened amid much fanfare in 1963. Over the years, this establishment kept adding buildings, so that the place is a hodge-

Lodging

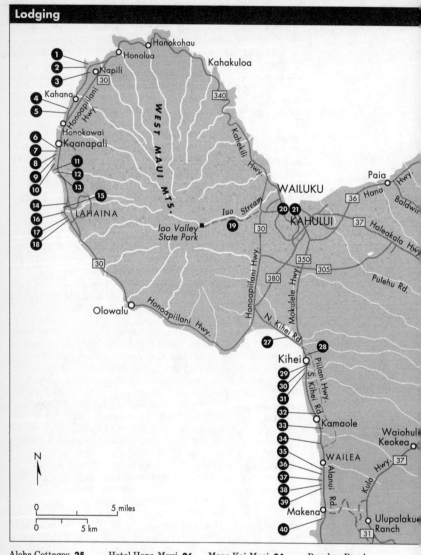

Aloha Cottages, **25**
Aston Kamaole Sands, **32**
Coconut Inn, **3**
Embassy Suites, **5**
Four Seasons Resort, **39**
Grand Hyatt Wailea, **38**
Hale Kamaole, **33**
Hana Kai-Maui, **24**
Heavenly Hana Inn, **23**

Hotel Hana-Maui, **26**
Hyatt Regency Maui, **13**
Iao Valley Lodge & Spring, **19**
Kaanapali Alii, **11**
Kaanapali Beach Hotel, **8**
Kapalua Bay Hotel, **1**
Koa Resort, **29**
Kula Lodge, **22**
Lahaina Hotel, **15**
Luana Kai Resort, **30**

Mana Kai-Maui, **34**
Maui Beach, **20**
Maui Inter-Continental Wailea, **37**
Maui Islander, **17**
Maui Lu Resort, **28**
Maui Marriott, **12**
Maui Palms, **21**
Maui Prince, **40**
Maui Sunset, **31**
Nani Kai Hale, **27**
Napili Kai Beach Club, **2**

Papakea Beach Resort, **4**
Pioneer Inn, **18**
Plantation Inn, **16**
Puunoa Beach Estates, **14**
Royal Lahaina, **6**
Sheraton Maui, **7**
Stouffer Wailea Beach Resort, **35**
Wailea Villas, **36**
Westin Maui, **10**
Whaler on Kaanapali Beach, **9**

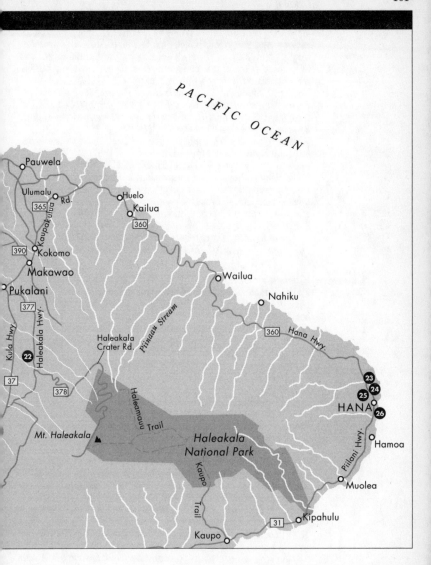

PACIFIC OCEAN

Pauwela

Ulumalu Rd.
365
Huelo
Kailua
360

390
Kokomo
Makawao
Pukalani
377
Wailua
Nahiku
Kula Hwy.
Haleakala Hwy.
360 Hana Hwy.
Haleakala
Crater Rd.
22
Piinaau Stream
378
23
24
Haleamauu Trail
25
HANA
26
Mt. Haleakala
Haleakala
National Park
Hamoa
Kaupo
Piilani Hwy.
Muolea
Trail
31
Kipahulu
Kaupo

podge architecturally, but the newly renovated interiors are more than comfortable. It does have one of Kaanapali's best locations, on a marvelous beach next to a black lava-rock promontory. Situated up on the rock are a restaurant and lounge, and even some guest units. The hotel offers a good luau that begins with a dramatic torch-lighting ceremony and a conch-shell blower at sundown. *Kaanapali Beach Resort, 2605 Kaanapali Pkwy., Lahaina 96761, tel. 808/661–0031 or 800/325–3535. 495 rooms with bath. Facilities: 2 restaurants, shops, tennis, golf, 2 pools, color TV, A/C. AE, DC, MC, V.*

Westin Maui. The Westin is another property from the developer of the Hyatt Maui. Opened in the fall of 1987, the Westin is a make-over of a lower-end hotel called the Maui Surf. The design restrictions inherent in a renovation, unfortunately, have limited the room size, which is rather small for the price. This, however, is a hotel for active people who like to be out and about and won't spend all their time in their rooms. *2365 Kaanapali Pkwy., Lahaina 96761, tel. 808/667–2525 or 800/228–3000. 761 rooms with bath. Beachfront. Facilities: 8 restaurants, lounges, shops, Jacuzzis, health club, beauty salon, 5 pools. AE, DC, MC, V.*

Expensive **Kaanapali Beach Hotel.** This property is right in the middle of all the Kaanapali action and offers much more reasonable rates than its neighbors. Instead of glitz and flash, you'll find a comfortable hotel with a friendly Hawaiian staff. The hotel conducts complimentary classes in hula, lei making, ukulele playing, and more. The renovation will most likely update the rooms. *2525 Kaanapali Pkwy., Lahaina 96761, tel. 808/661–0011 or 800/657–7700. 430 rooms with bath. Beachfront. Facilities: pool, golf, shops, color TV, A/C, restaurants, lounge. AE, DC, MC, V.*

★ **Napili Kai Beach Club.** Owner Dorothy Millar and her late husband created a homey little place on one of the finest beaches in Maui; it attracts a loyal following each year. The clean, Japanese-style rooms with shoji doors open onto your lanai, with the beach and ocean right outdoors. This place is particularly popular with honeymooners and Canadians. The weekly cocktail party Mrs. Millar continues to host encourages a friendly atmosphere. *5900 Honoapiilani Hwy., Lahaina 96761, tel. 808/669–6271 or 800/367–5030. 163 rooms with bath. Beachfront. Facilities: 4 pools, Jacuzzi, tennis courts, putting green. No credit cards. Advance payment or traveler's checks required.*

Royal Lahaina. Ever since California wholesaling giant Pleasant Hawaiian Holidays (PHH) purchased this 540-room property there have been plans to renovate. Now Outrigger Hotels has taken over management, and "renovate" is its middle name. The lanais will continue to have their stunning ocean or golf-course views, which are worth the price of the room. What distinguishes the Royal Lahaina are the two-story ocean cottages, each divided into four units. Lushly decorated, the bedrooms open to the trade winds on two sides. The upstairs units have private lanais, while the downstairs share. *2780 Kekaa Dr., Lahaina 96761, tel. 808/661–3611 or 800/733–7777. 540 rooms with bath. Beachfront. Facilities: 3 pools, shops, 3 restaurants, tennis, golf, color TV, A/C. AE, DC, MC, V.*

Whaler on Kaanapali Beach. In its twin 12-story towers, this hotel offers 3 good-size unit configurations, from studios to two-bedrooms, all smartly decorated and air-conditioned, and many of the amenities that are real finds in condominium complexes—a 24-hour front desk, tennis courts, an exercise room and sauna, and a small sundries store. Units are elegantly furnished, with tropical prints. The best thing about the Whaler, however, is its location, right on one of the state's finest beaches, between the Kaanapali Beach Hotel and Whalers Village Shopping Center. Restaurants, golf, and tennis are nearby. *2481 Kaanapali Pkwy., Lahaina 96761, tel. 808/661–4861 or 800/367–7052. 360 studio, 1- and 2-bedroom condo units with bath on Kaanapali Beach. Facilities: pool, shops, A/C, color TV, tennis, golf, gym, sauna, Jacuzzi. AE, MC, V.*

Moderate
★ **Coconut Inn.** Although the management has changed, this hotel is still highly recommended. The Coconut Inn was a dumpy apartment building until California financial whiz George Gilman bought it and turned it into a small, personal country inn. Gilman has since sold out and opened a similar property called the Coconut Plaza in Waikiki, but the Coconut Inn retains much of its charm. The transformed hotel suites (once one-bedroom apartments) each come with a kitchen. A free-form pool and stream are located in the center courtyard, where guests congregate and become acquainted. The complimentary breakfast is served each morning in the lobby area. This is a comfortable place, and most people don't mind the trek to the beach. *181 Hui Rd. F, Napili 96761, tel. 808/669–5712 or 800/367–8006. 40 1-bedroom units with bath and kitchens. About ½ mi from beach. Facilities: pool, spa, color TV, Continental breakfast, daily maid service. MC, V.*

Lahaina Hotel. This once derelict hotel has reopened after more than $3 million in renovations by Honolulu businessmen Rick Ralston and Alan Beall. Ralston, also responsible for the rebirth of the Manoa Valley Inn on Oahu, has stocked the 13-room Maui property with antique beds, wardrobes, and chests, as well as delightful country print curtains and spreads. Downstairs, the trendy David Paul's Lahaina Grill, near the lively corner of Front Street and Lahainaluna Road, attracts diners. *127 Lahainaluna Rd., Lahaina 96761, tel. 808/661–0577 or 800/669–3444. 13 rooms with bath. MC, V.*

Maui Islander. An alternative to the pricey West Maui resorts, located in a quieter section of Lahaina, a few blocks from the ocean. Set on a 10-acre jungle site filled with palms, banana trees, plumeria trees, and torch ginger, the hotel has nine two-story buildings with large studios and even bigger one-bedrooms. Upstairs rooms have high, open-beam ceilings. Each morning guests are served complimentary coffee. *660 Wainee St., Lahaina 96761, tel. 808/667–9766 or 800/367–5226. 372 rooms with bath. Facilities: pool, tennis, color TV, A/C, ceiling fans, daily maid service, 24-hour front desk. AE, DC, MC, V.*

Papakea Beach Resort. This resort is an active place to stay if you consider all the classes held here, such as swimming, snorkeling, and pineapple cutting. Located in Honokowai, Papakea has built-in privacy because its units are spread out among 11 low-rise buildings on some 13 acres of land. You aren't really aware that you're sharing the property with 363 other rooms. Bamboo-lined walkways between buildings and fish-stocked ponds create a serene mood. *3481 Lower Honoapiilani Hwy., Lahaina 96761, tel. 808/661–7133 or 800/367–5637. 364 units with bath, including studios and 1- and 2-bedrooms. Beachfront. Facilities: 2 pools, whirlpool, spas, saunas, color TV, tennis, putting green. AE, MC, V.*

★ **Plantation Inn.** A nine-room property, the Plantation Inn is one of those places you just won't find everywhere else. The newly constructed inn resembles a renovated Victorian home on a quiet country street in the heart of Lahaina, within walking distance of the ocean and all the down-to-earth bars, restaurants, and shops in the old whaling port. Each room at the inn is decorated differently, with exquisite attention to detail. The owners have stocked the place with antiques, stained glass, brass beds, and ceiling fans and polished up the hardwood floors, wood trim, and wide verandas. Downstairs is one of Hawaii's best French restaurants, Gerard's, whose candlelit ambience definitely adds to the romantic European charm of the place. The Plantation Inn also offers meal, airfare, car, and dive packages. *174 Lahainaluna Rd., Lahaina 96761, tel. 808/ 667–9225 or 800/433–6815. 9 rooms with bath; suite available. Facilities: restaurant, refrigerators, pool, A/C, ceiling fans, color TV. AE, MC, V.*

Inexpensive **Pioneer Inn.** You want fancy? Don't check into the Pioneer Inn. If, however, you'd like to try a taste of old Lahaina, then this is the place for you. Downstairs is the boisterous saloon, where tourists and locals alike hang out—if you get a room over the bar, forget about sleeping until the bartender rousts the last revelers at about 1 AM. Rooms are on the second floor. In the older section up front, they're nothing fancy: smallish and rather dim, with ceiling fans and no air-conditioning. Ask about the Spencer Tracy–Katharine Hepburn suite in the newer section, which is brighter and quieter, with air-conditioning. In this newer wing, some rooms overlook the small hotel pool and court-yard, while others face Front Street. What you get at the Pioneer Inn is history—and plenty of it. *658 Wharf St., Lahaina 96761, tel. 808/661–3636. 48 rooms with bath. Near the ocean. Facilities: 2 restaurants, cocktail lounge, small pool. AE, DC, MC, V.*

Central Maui

Moderate **Maui Beach.** Like its next-door neighbor the Maui Palms, this hotel has no-frills accommodations. You'll get a room with modest furnishings. The restaurant isn't bad, however, and you can find specials that are pretty tasty. Free airport shuttle service is provided. *170 Kaahumanu Ave., Kahului 96732, tel. 808/ 877–0051 or 800/367–5004. 154 rooms with bath, on the bay. Facilities: restaurant, shops, pool, A/C. AE, DC, MC, V.*

Inexpensive **Iao Valley Lodge & Spring.** This is one of those word-of-mouth places that's never very busy, perhaps because it has only seven rooms. Recently renovated, the accommodations are modern and new, but don't expect the elegant tropical haven you'll find in some of the resort areas. The setting is fantastic: a private mountain valley far away from traffic or noise. The popular Mark Edison's restaurant (*see* Chapter 6) may be found nearby, with live music on occasion. *For reservations, write to RR 1, Box 518, Wailuku 96793, tel. 808/242–5555. 7 rooms with bath. Room-and-car package available. MC, V.*

Maui Palms. Although this is probably one of the best buys in Central Maui (at least in a place where you can be assured of safety), don't get too excited. What you get here is a simple room with very basic furnishings. Some rooms are right on Kahului Bay, but that doesn't add much to the ambience because the windows are mostly shuttered. The hotel's proximity to the airport and major shopping areas, however, can't be beat. *170 Kaahumanu Ave., Kahului 96732, tel. 808/877–0071 or 800/367–5004. 103 rooms with bath. Facilities: pool, shops, restaurant, cocktail lounge, TV. Some rooms with A/C. AE, DC, MC, V.*

East Maui

Very Expensive **Four Seasons Resort.** Opened in mid-1990, the Four Seasons has
★ quickly become a favorite Maui hotel. Part of the reason is its location: smack dab on one of the Valley Island's finest beaches with all the amenities of the well-groomed Wailea Resort. The property itself is no less a stunner, with terraces, courtyards, gardens, waterfalls, and fountains. Nearly all the rooms have an ocean view and combine traditional style with tropical touches. You'll find terry-cloth robes and Japanese yukatas in each room. The service here is the best in Hawaii. *3900 Wailea Alanui, Wailea 96753, tel. 808/874–8000 or 800/334–MAUI. 380 rooms with bath. Facilities: 3 restaurants, cocktail lounges, tennis, golf, nearby shopping, pool, health club. AE, DC, MC, V.*

Grand Hyatt Wailea. This brand new hotel has pretty much taken over the quiet Wailea beach with its opulent water features, gardens, and art work. Built for some $600 million, the 787-room hotel features a 2,000-foot river pool with rapids, slides and rocks, as well as a regular pool that turns into a lighted fountain at night. Hawaii's largest spa is located at the Grand Hyatt and offers massages, facials, mud baths, weight training, steam rooms, milk baths, and more. There are also facilities for weddings and child care. The Hyatt has outdone itself in guest rooms, installing three telephones per unit, large marble baths and separate showers. While here, guests can dine in a Japanese restaurant, enjoy seafood dockside, or take in panoramic views from the main dining room. *Wailea Alanui Dr., Wailea, 96753, tel. 808/875–1234. 787 rooms with bath. Beachfront. Facilities: pools, spa, restaurants, shops, cocktail lounges, TV, A/C. AE, DC, MC, V.*

★ **Hotel Hana-Maui.** One of the best places to stay in Hawaii—if not the Western Hemisphere—is this small, secluded hotel in Hana. A few years ago, the Rosewood Corporation of Dallas purchased the hotel and the 7,000-acre ranch that surrounds it. It then proceeded to invest an additional $25 million or so in upgrading the hotel before selling it to a Japanese investor. The buildings now boast white plaster walls and trellised verandas, while inside, the rooms have bleached wood floors, overstuffed furniture in natural fabrics, and such decorator touches as art and orchids. Sheraton Hotels has recently taken over the management of this hotel, and they have continued to upgrade amenities and decor. *Box 8, Hana 96713, tel. 808/248–8211, or 800/321–HANA. 97 large units with bath. Facilities: shuttle to secluded beach, pool, shops, restaurant, cocktail lounge, tennis, stables, library, jogging paths. All meals included in rates. AE, DC, MC, V.*

Maui Inter-Continental Wailea. Many repeat guests swear an undying loyalty to the Inter-Continental, coming back year after year to prove it. Luxurious without being overwhelming, this is a genuine hotel—upscale, unpretentious, and expertly run, with its share of amenities, including a set of rooms right on the beach. All the quietly elegant rooms are decorated in subtle tones of white, peach, or lavender and have private lanais and spacious bathrooms. The grounds are beautiful, with walks along paths through jungles of palm, banana, and torch ginger (a red-blossomed tropical flower). Activities abound here, and award-winning restaurants are located within the hotel. *3700 Wailea Alanui, Wailea 96753, tel. 808/879–1922 or 800/367–2960. 550 rooms with bath. Beachfront. Facilities: golf, tennis, restaurants, pools, Jacuzzi, shops. AE, DC, MC, V.*

Maui Prince. The Prince is a low-key luxury hotel, quietly attending to upscale hospitality since its opening in 1986. The attention to service, style, and presentation are apparent from the minute you walk into the delightful open-air lobby of the hotel, which is owned and managed by a Japanese company. Rooms on three levels surround the courtyard, which is home to a Japanese garden with carefully tended plants and a bubbling stream. Each evening a three-piece string ensemble performs classical music in the courtyard. Rooms are not elaborately decorated—instead, they're rather understated, in tones of mauve and beige. Unfortunately, there's an earth berm between the hotel and the beach—part of the agreement the hotel had to make with the zoning commission and local residents—so an ocean view isn't possible from the first floor. *5400 Makena Alanui Rd., Kihei 96753, tel. 808/874–1111 or 800/321–MAUI. 300 rooms with bath. Beachfront. Facilities: 4 restaurants, pool, golf, tennis, shops, color TV, A/C. AE, DC, MC, V.*

★ **Stouffer Wailea Beach Resort.** This is the first hotel you'll come to once you enter the stylish Wailea Beach Resort. Nothing here is lean. Situated on fantastic Mokapu Beach, most of the hotel's luxury rooms are contained in a seven-story, T-shape building, and the Mokapu Beach Club—26 cottagelike suites—is right on the water. Guest rooms, decorated in beige, burgundy, and blue, have refrigerators. The hotel emphasizes Hawaiian flavor, with gigantic contemporary tapestries and gorgeous carpets in the public areas; outside, you'll find gardens of exotic flowers, waterfalls, and reflecting ponds. Plenty of activities and award-winning restaurants are available right on the property. *3550 Wailea Alanui Dr., Wailea 96753, tel. 808/879–4900 or 800/9–WAILEA. 347 rooms with bath. Beachfront. Facilities: pool, Jacuzzi, restaurants, shops, cocktail lounges, color TV with HBO, A/C. AE, DC, MC, V.*

Expensive **Wailea Villas.** The Wailea Resort has built three fine condominiums, calling them—appropriately—Wailea Ekahi, Wailea Elua, and Wailea Ekolu (Wailea One, Two, and Three). All three have beautifully landscaped grounds, large units with exceptional views, and access to one of the island's best beaches. Wailea Elua is usually considered the nicest of the three, with more expensive furnishings and rates to match. We recommend all three. It's an expansive property, with all the amenities of the fine Wailea Resort, including daily maid service and a concierge. *3750 Wailea Alanui Dr., Wailea 96753, tel. 808/879–1595 or 800/367–5246. 598 units in 3 complexes, 2 of them beachfront. 1-, 2-, and 3-bedroom apartments with bath available. Facilities: pools, color TV, hotel restaurants and lounges nearby. MC, V.*

Moderate **Aston Kamaole Sands.** This is a huge property for Kihei—10 four-story buildings wrap around a grassy slope on which are clustered swimming and wading pools, a small waterfall, Jacuzzis, and barbecues. All units have laundry facilities but no air-conditioning. Managed by the well-run Aston Hotels & Resorts, this condominium property boasts a 24-hour front desk, an Activities Desk, and on-property food and beverage. *2695 S. Kihei Rd., Kihei 96753, tel. 808/874–8700 or 800/92–ASTON. 440 1-, 2-, and 3-bedroom condo units with bath. Across the road from Kihei Beach. Facilities: pool, jet spa, wading pool, tennis. AE, DC, MC, V.*

Hale Kamaole. The beach is within strolling distance right across the road. This property has eight buildings set in a U shape to capture the best ocean views, and there's an attractive lawn. *2737 S. Kihei Rd., Kihei 96753, tel. 808/879–2698 or 800/ 367–2970. 187 1- and 2-bedroom condo units with bath. Facilities: pool, tennis, color TV, A/C. No credit cards.*

★ **Hana Kai-Maui.** This small condominium is the only true beachfront property in the tiny town of Hana. The large and simply furnished units are set on lush, manicured grounds. One added benefit is the spring-fed swimming pool on one side of the property: It was built with lava rock and looks almost too unusual to swim in. *Box 38, Hana 96713, tel. 808/248–8426 or 808/248–7742. 17 units with bath. Beachfront. AE, MC, V.*

Koa Resort. This establishment's five two-story buildings cluster around a beautiful lawn that serves as a putting green. Rooms are large and tropically furnished in bamboo and rattan; lanais are lush with bougainvillea. The huge 120-foot-long pool is spanned by a bridge, with Kihei's only diving board. This reasonably priced property is as nice as you'll find in Kaanapali. *811 S. Kihei Rd., Kihei 96753, tel. 808/879–1161. 54 1-, 2-, and 3-bedroom units with bath near the beach. Facilities: pool, Jacuzzi, TV, tennis, shuffleboard, spa, putting green, barbecue. MC, V.*

Kula Lodge. The Kula Lodge isn't your typical Hawaiian place, for two reasons: (1) it looks like a chalet property that should grace the Swiss Alps; and (2) three of its five units come with a fireplace. But the lodge is charming and cozy in spite of its nontropical ambience. It's a perfect spot for a romantic interlude or reading a good book next to a roaring fire. The five units are in two wooden cabins; four of them have lofts in addition to the ample bed space downstairs. Set on 3 wooded acres, the lodge has a view of the valley and ocean, enhanced even more by the forest that surrounds it. Other amenities include a restaurant and lounge, as well as a gift shop and a protea co-op that will pack the unusual flowers for you to take home. The rates include breakfast. *RR1, Box 475, Kula 96790, tel. 808/878–1535. 5 units with bath. Facilities: restaurant. No phones or TVs. MC, V.*

Luana Kai Resort. This condo, right on the beach, boasts a lovely view. The buildings are widely separated, enabling guests to have privacy. The property has tennis courts, two saunas, a putting green, and a hot tub. Rooms are decorated with rattan furnishings and tropical prints, and you also get a loft in the two- and three-bedroom units. *940 S. Kihei Rd., Kihei 96753, tel. 808/879–1268 or 800/669–1127. 114 1-, 2-, and 3-bedroom condominiums with bath. Facilities: pool, tennis, Jacuzzi. AE, MC, V.*

★ **Mana Kai-Maui.** This lodging is a real find in Kihei, partly because of the property itself and partly because it sits on the end of one of the nicest beaches in the state, just down the strip from the Stouffer Wailea. Here you can get a studio without a kitchen, or a one- or two-bedroom unit with a kitchen. The decor is modest—what people in the Islands might call typical tropical—but the view of the ocean right outside the lanai overcomes any reservations you might have about the rooms' interiors. What's more, the rates usually include a car. The Mana Kai has a very good beachfront restaurant, open for all meals. *2960 S. Kihei Rd., Kihei 96753, tel. 808/879–1561 or 800/525–2025. 140 rooms. Beachfront. Facilities: pool, restaurant, lounge, shopping arcade, cable color TV, ceiling fans. AE, DC, MC, V.*

Maui Lu Resort. The first hotel in Kihei, this place reminds one of a rustic lodge. The main lobby was the summer home of the original owner, and over the years, the Maui Lu has added numerous wooden buildings and cottages to its 28 acres. Of the 170 rooms, 50 are right on the beach, in their own secluded area. The rest are across Kihei Road, on the main property. In addition, 16 large, one-bedroom cottages have a garden setting and screened-in lanais. The decor isn't fancy, but it isn't motel-tacky either. *575 S. Kihei Rd., Kihei 96753, tel. 808/879–5881 or 800/92–ASTON. 170 rooms with bath. Facilities: restaurant, lounge, pool, shops, color TV, A/C, tennis. AE, DC, MC, V.*

Maui Sunset. If you want to get in shape on your vacation, this is the place. It boasts one of the only health spas in a Kihei condo. It has a sauna and whirlpool for soaking away post-exercise aches and pains, as well as a variety of other activities for the sports-minded. You have a choice of spacious one-, two-, and three-bedroom units, which have been decorated in pleasant pastels and are located in two five-story concrete-block buildings. *1032 S. Kihei Rd., Kihei 96753, tel. 808/879–0674 or 800/843–5880. 225 condominiums with bath, on the beach. Facilities: pool, tennis, volleyball, shuffleboard, putting green, A/C. No credit cards for rooms; prepayment required.*

Inexpensive **Aloha Cottages.** If you want to meet the people in little Hana town, check into one of these cottages, run by Fusae Nakamura. Tourism is Mrs. Nakamura's way of earning extra money for her family now that she's retired, and she takes it seriously. The three two-bedroom units and one studio all have kitchens. The rooms are sparsely furnished but clean and adequate. A special touch are the carefully tended fruit trees on the neighboring property—Mrs. Nakamura often supplies her guest with the harvest, which includes papaya, bananas, and avocados. *Hana 96713, tel. 808/248–8420. 4 cottages with bath. No credit cards.*

Heavenly Hana Inn. Whether you fly or drive to Hana, you'll pass the Heavenly Hana Inn and probably wonder what it is. An impressive Japanese gate flanked by two lions guards the property, making it look like a temple of sorts. Inside, the rustic and quiet inn goes in for eccentric decor, with knickknacks everywhere. You can rent one of four two-bedroom units, each with a kitchenette and decorated with Japanese shoji screens, antique furniture, and Asian art. If the location, 2 miles from town, seems too remote (although, let's face it, all of Hana is remote), the inn also has a one-bedroom beach cottage and a family cottage near the center of town. *Box 146, Hana 96713, tel. 808/248–8442. 4 rooms, plus 1 cottage on Hana Bay and 1 in town. Kitchenettes, lanais, TVs. No credit cards.*

Nani Kai Hale. This property, at the head of a seemingly endless beach, consists of six stories of condominium units (as well as rooms without kitchens) in sparkling white buildings. Nani Kai Hale has a better-than-average pool and a nice lawn out back, but its main attraction is all that glorious sand. Although there are no restaurants, dining and groceries may be found within a mile. No phones are available, except for long-term guests. *73 N. Kihei Rd., Kihei 96753, tel. 808/879–9120 or 800/ 367–6032. 46 condo units with bath, on the beach. Some hotel rooms available; other units are studios, 1-, and 2-bedrooms, with kitchens. Facilities: pool; some rooms with TV. No credit cards.*

Bed-and-Breakfasts

Maui also has quite a few homes available for bed-and-breakfast rentals. Many have their units in separate guest houses, which allows privacy while still giving you a chance to get to know your hosts. Rates range from $30 a night to as much as $150. For more information about Maui B&Bs, write or phone:

Bed & Breakfast Hawaii (Box 449, Kapaa 96746, tel. 808/822–7771 or 800/733–1632). Headquartered on Kauai, this organization has listings throughout the state and handles about 35 B&Bs on Maui. A directory is available for $10.95.

Bed & Breakfast Honolulu (3242 Kaohinani Dr., Honolulu 96817, tel. 800/288–4666). This organization has statewide listings, with about 50 B&Bs, or nearly 100 units, on Maui.

Bed & Breakfast Maui-Style (Box 98, Kihei 96784, tel. 808/879–7865 or 800/848–5567). This organization has listings for about 25 B&Bs in Maui.

House Rentals

You can rent a house on Maui through several brokers. There is no average rate; you can expect to find homes for as little as $100 a night or as much as $1,000. By writing to the following management companies, you can get more information on specific homes, including brochures with photographs and details of the types of properties.

Premier Connections of Hawaii (1993 S. Kihei Rd., Suite 209, Kihei 96753, tel. 808/329–6284).

Villas of Hawaii (4218 Waialae Ave., Suite 203, Honolulu 96816, tel. 800/522–3030).

Windsurfing West Ltd. (Box 330104, Kahului 96733, tel. 800/ 782–6105).

Hostels

Maui's one youth hostel is in a secluded location, which makes it very inconvenient for a typical bargain hunter (most likely a student), who may not have a car. Run by the YMCA, the hostel is a rustic wooden building situated on a beautiful peninsula nearly 35 miles from the airport. A separate bathhouse with hot showers is available, and men and women bunk separately, dorm style. Check in between 4 and 6 PM, and bring a bedroll. The maximum stay is five nights. For more information, write to: **YMCA** (Box 820, Wailuku 96793, tel. 808/244–3253). Cost: under $10 per night.

8 The Arts and Nightlife

The Arts

Most of Maui's cultural activities are community efforts, with theater, film, and symphony productions held in the island's central towns of Kahului and Wailuku. For more specific information, check the daily newspaper, the *Maui News*.

Film

International Film Festival. This acclaimed salute to celluloid used to be restricted to Honolulu, but now festival films are also presented in Maui. Each year in late November and early December, the festival, sponsored by East-West Center, brings together filmmakers from Asia, the Pacific Rim, and the United States to view feature films, documentaries, and shorts. The films are shown at the Holiday Theaters at the Kaahumanu Center. To find out about specific films and dates, phone the East-West Center's International Film Festival Office (tel. 808/944–7200) in Honolulu.

Music

Kapalua Music Festival. Since 1982, the music festival has brought some of the world's finest musicians to Maui for several days each summer. Representatives from Juilliard and the Chicago and New York philharmonics, the Tokyo String Quartet, Israeli-born musical director Yishak Schotten, and violinist Joseph Swensen are only a few of those who've performed here in recent years. Kapalua usually has special room rates during the festival. *J. Walter Cameron Center, 95 Mahalani St., Wailuku 96793, tel. 808/244–3771. Tickets: $10 adults, $6 children 6–12.*

Maui Philharmonic Society. Now entering its 49th season, the Society has recently presented such prestigious performers as Ballet Hispanico, Shostakovich String Quartet, and the new-age pianist Philip Glass. Performances are held in various spots around the island. *J. Walter Cameron Center, 95 Mahalani St., Wailuku 96793, tel. 808/244–3771.*

Maui Symphony Orchestra The symphony orchestra performs five season concerts and a few special musical sensations as well, including a July 4th concert on the Kaanapali Golf Course, complete with fireworks. The regular season includes a Christmas concert, an opera gala, a classical concert, and two pops concerts outdoors at Wailea. *Tel. 808/244–5439. Season tickets: $12 adults, $8 students; tickets for the July 4th concert: $3 adults, $1 children.*

Theater

Baldwin Theatre Guild. Dramas, comedies, and musicals for the entire island are presented by this group about eight times a year. The guild has staged such favorites as *The Glass Menagerie, Brigadoon,* and *The Miser.* Musicals are held in the Community Auditorium, which seats 1,200, while all other plays are presented in the Baldwin High School Mini Theatre. *1650 Kaahumanu Ave., Kahului, tel. 808/242–5821. Tickets: $6 adults, $4 seniors, $3 students.*

Maui Community Theatre. Now staging about six plays a year, this is the oldest dramatic group on the island, started in the early 1900s. Last season's productions included *Fiddler on the*

Roof, Amadeus, and *Dracula: The Musical?* Each July, the
group also holds a fund-raising variety show, which can be a
hoot. *Iao Theatre, 68 N. Market, Wailuku, tel. 808/242–6969.
Tickets for musicals: $10 adults, $9 seniors, $5 children under
17. Nonmusicals are $1 less.*

Maui Youth Theatre. This theater program for children is one of
the largest arts organizations in Hawaii; it takes plays into the
schools around the county but also performs about 10 productions a year for the entire community. Plays have included
name shows, such as *Mame,* and original plays and ethnic dramas. Performances are held in various locations around the island. *Box 518, Puunene 96784, tel. 808/871–7484; box office 808/
871–6516. Tickets: $3–$8.*

Nightlife

Nightlife on Maui can be of the make-your-own-fun variety. As
on all the Neighbor Islands, the pace is a bit slower than what
you'll find in Waikiki. Watching the sunset from a tropical
perch, taking a moonlight stroll along one of the island's near-
perfect crescent beaches, or dining in a meadow can be some of
the best nightlife you'll find.

Dancing, luaus, dinner cruises, and so on are found mainly in
the resort areas. Kaanapali in particular can really get hop-
ping, with myriad activities for visitors of all ages. The old
whaling port of Lahaina also parties with the best of them, and
attracts a younger, often tow-headed crowd who all seem to be
visiting from towns on the West Coast. Overall, Wailea and
Kapalua appear more sedate, but Wailea's Maui Inter-Continental boasts one of the island's most lively discos, the Inu Inu
Lounge, which always seems jammed.

Bars and Clubs

Comedy **Comedy Club** (Maui Marriott, Kaanapali Beach Resort, tel.
808/667–1200). Every Sunday evening is laugh night at the
Marriott now that the owners of the Honolulu Comedy Club
have set up a weekly Valley Isle venue. Although the show
starts at 8 AM in the Lobby Bar, it's better to get there early
since comedy has caught on in a big way. Tickets are $10.

Contemporary **El Crab Catcher** (Whalers Village, Kaanapali, tel. 808/661–
Music 4423). In addition to seafood, you'll find live music here nightly,
5:30–7:30. Often a contemporary Hawaiian duo or trio per-
forms.

Lost Horizon (3550 Wailea Alanui Dr., Wailea, tel. 808/879–
4900). This popular spot in the Stouffer Wailea Beach Resort
features live easy-listening music, often Hawaiian. There's
some dancing here, but it's on the slow side.

Molokini Lounge (Maui Prince Hotel, Makena Resort, tel. 808/
874–1111). This is a pleasant bar with an ocean view, and you
can even see Molokini Island before the sun goes down. Live
music is presented, often Hawaiian in theme. There's a dance
floor for late-night revelry.

Discos **Banana Moon** (Maui Marriott, Kaanapali Beach Resort, tel.
808/667–1200). This is a lively spot in the Maui Marriott Hotel,
open nightly from 9 to 2. It has high-tech decor and good music.
Banana Moon is an enjoyable place to meet other young tourists
and hotel employees out for a night on the town.

Inu Inu Lounge (Maui Inter-Continental Wailea, Wailea Resort, tel. 808/879–1922). There's dancing nightly here starting at 9, with live music—rock, big bands, or golden oldies. This is a very active spot for young crowds from Wailea, Kihei, and Makena. It also lures groups who are visiting the resort.

Moose McGillycuddy's (844 Front St., Lahaina, tel. 808/667–7758). The Moose has only recorded music, but it's played so loud you would swear it's live. This entertaining place tends to draw an early-20s crowd, who come for the burgers and beer and to meet one another.

Spats II (Hyatt Regency Maui, Kaanapali Beach Resort, tel. 808/667–7474). This club is open for disco dancing Sunday through Thursday 10 AM –2 AM and Fridays and Saturdays until 4. (Spats is a Travel-Holiday Award–winning Italian restaurant from 6:30 to 9:30.) There's a cover charge on Friday and Saturday nights.

Jazz **Blackie's Bar** (Blackie's Boat Yard, on the mountain side of Honoapiilani Hwy. in an orange octagonal building, Lahaina, tel. 808/667–7979). Even without the finest jazz on Maui, Blackie's would be an interesting place to go. Take Blackie himself; the crusty proprietor often cruises the joint, making sure everyone's behaving, and chastising those who put their feet on the chairs or spit or break some other rule he has set forth for his establishment. The jazz is terrific, featuring the Gene Argel Trio and other guest performers. The music stops at 8, however, because that's when Blackie goes to bed.

Dinner and Sunset Cruises

Stardancer. This 150-foot luxury yacht is the largest to sail the Lahaina waters, serving nightly a gourmet buffet in its elegant dining room. The three-level boat also has a disco. *Lahaina Harbor, Lahaina 96761, tel. 808/871–1144. Cost: $50.*

Genesis Sailing Charters. This dinner sail goes for 2½ hours and includes a gourmet catered meal on the 48-foot luxury sailing yacht *Genesis*. The cruise is limited to 20 passengers at a time. *Box 10697, Lahaina 96761, tel. 808/667–5667. Cost: $56 adults.*

Pardner Sailing Charters. Six passengers at a time are taken for a two-hour sunset sail with champagne, mai tais, and snacks on the 46-foot ketch the *Pardner. Pier 21, Lahaina Harbor, Lahaina 96767, tel. 808/661–3448. Cost: $30 adults.*

Scotch Mist Charters. A two-hour champagne sunset sail is offered on the 19-passenger Santa Cruz 50 sloop *Scotch Mist II. Box 831, Lahaina 96767, tel. 808/661–0386. Cost: $30 adults.*

Windjammer Cruises. This cruise includes a sit-down meal and live entertainment on the 65-foot, 110-passenger *Spirit of Windjammer*, a three-masted schooner. *505 Front St., Suite 229, Lahaina 96761, tel. 808/667–6834. Cost: $49 adults.*

Luaus and Polynesian Revues

Drums of the Pacific. The Hyatt presents a fine Polynesian revue on the hotel's Sunset Terrace. The all-you-can-eat buffet dinner includes such fare as fresh fish, prime rib, chicken, and a native luau pupu platter. Afterward, the show features traditional dances and chants from such countries as Tahiti, Samoa, and New Zealand. *Hyatt Regency Maui, Kaanapali, tel. 808/ 661–1234, ext. 4420. Tickets: $42 adults, $34 children 6–12. Mon.-Wed., Fri., Sat. Dinner seating begins at 5:30.*

Luau at the Maui Lu. Held on Saturday evenings only on the grounds of the Maui Lu Resort, this standard Maui event includes an imu ceremony, a Polynesian buffet dinner, all the drink you want, and a Polynesian revue. *Maui Lu Resort, 575 S. Kihei Rd., Kihei, tel. 808/879–5881. Cost: $35 adults, $20.50 children 7–12.*

Maui's Merriest Luau. The Inter-Continental's oceanfront lawn is certainly a beautiful spot to hold a luau. The traditional feast begins with a rum punch welcome and imu ceremony, and the evening includes colorful Polynesian entertainment. *Maui InterContinental Wailea, Wailea, tel. 808/879–1922. Tues. and Thurs. 5:30.*

Old Lahaina Luau. This is the best luau you'll find on Maui—it's small, personal, and authentic. The Old Lahaina Luau is held on the beach at 505 Front Street in Lahaina, presumably the former Hawaiian entertainment grounds of the royals. You'll get all-you-can-eat traditional Hawaiian luau food: kalua (roasted) pork, long rice, lomi salmon, haupia cake, and other items, such as fresh fruit and salad. You'll also get all you can drink. Guests sit either on tatami mats or at tables. Then there's the entertainment, featuring a musical journey from Old Hawaii to the present with hula, chanting, and singing. Four young men started the Old Lahaina Luau in 1986, and their attention to detail is remarkable. *505 Front St., Lahaina, tel. 808/667–1998. Tickets: $45 adults, $25 children under 13, infants free.*

Stouffer Wailea Beach Resort Luau. A five-star hotel, the Stouffer puts on its excellent Hawaiian luau each Monday and Thursday evening, featuring an open bar, an imu ceremony, a luau buffet, music by a Hawaiian band, and a show called "Memories of the Pacific," featuring dancers performing pieces from around the Pacific—including one wielding a "fire knife." *Stouffer Wailea Beach Resort, 3550 Wailea Alanui Dr., tel. 808/ 879–4900. Cost: $38 adults, $21 children under 12.*

Shows

Maui Tropical Plantation's Hawaiian Country Barbecue & Buddy Fo Revue. This Hawaiian country evening with a *paniolo* (cowboy) theme starts with a narrated tram ride through about half of the 120-acre showcase of Hawaii's leading agricultural crops; then it moves to an all-you-can-eat barbecued steak dinner and open bar. After, Buddy Fo and his lively entertainers put on a Hawaiian country-and-western variety show; the audience can join in for some square dancing. *Maui Tropical Plantation, Wailuku, tel. 808/244–7643. Tickets: $46.95 adults, $23.50 children 5–12, $10 children under 5. Mon., Wed., Fri. 5–8 PM.*

Hawaiian Vocabulary

The Hawaiian language is unlike anything heard by the average traveler. But given the chance, say at a traditional church service or a local ritual ceremony, visitors will find the soft, rolling language of the Islands both interesting and refreshing to the ear.

Although an understanding of Hawaiian is by no means required on a trip to the Aloha State, *malihinis*, or newcomers, will find plenty of opportunities to pick up a few of the local words and phrases. In fact, traditional names and expressions are still in such wide usage today that visitors will be hard pressed not to read or hear them each day of their visit. Such exposure enriches a stay in Hawaii. With a basic understanding and some uninhibited practice, anyone can have enough command of the local tongue to ask for directions and to order off the neighborhood restaurant menu.

Simplifying the learning process is the fact that the Hawaiian language contains only seven consonants—H, K, L, M, N, P, and W—and the five vowels. All syllables and all words end in a vowel. Each vowel, with the exception of diphthongized double vowels such as *au* (pronounced ow) or *ai* (pronounced eye), is pronounced separately. *Aa*, the word for "rough lava" for example, is pronounced ah-ah.

Although some Hawaiian words have only vowels, most also contain some combination consonants as well. Consonants are never doubled, and they always begin syllables, as in Ka-me-ha-me-ha.

The accent in most Hawaiian words falls on the next-to-the-last, or penultimate, syllable. Examples are KO-na, PA-li and KA-na. The exception occurs when the vowels in the second syllable become dipthongized, as in ha-PAI and ma-KAI, which are fundamentally ha-PA-i and ma-KA-i.

Pronounciation is simple. Use the following table as a guide:

Pronounce *A* "uh" as in above; *E* "ay" as in weigh; *I* "ee" as in marine; *O* "oh" as in no; *U* "oo" as in true.

Consonants mirror their English equivalents, with the exception of W. When the letter begins the last syllable of a word, it is sometimes pronounced as a V. Awa, the Polynesian drink, is pronounced "ava"; Ewa is pronounced "Eva."

What follows is a glossary of some of the most commonly used Hawaiian words. Don't be afraid to give them a try. Hawaiian residents appreciate visitors who at least try to pick up the local language—no matter how fractured the pronunciation.

aa—rough, crumbling lava, contrasting with *pahoehoe*, which is smooth.
ae—yes.
akamai—smart, clever, possessing savoir-faire.
ala—a road, path, or trail.
alii—a Hawaiian chief, a member of the chiefly class; also plural.

aloha—love, affection, kindness. Also a salutation meaning both greetings and farewell.

aole—no.

auwai—a ditch.

auwe—alas, woe is me!

ehu—a red-haired Hawaiian.

ewa—in the direction of Ewa plantation, west of Honolulu.

hala—the pandanus tree, whose leaves *(lauhala)* are used to make baskets and plaited mats.

hale—a house.

hana—to work.

haole—originally a stranger or foreigner. Since the first foreigners were Caucasian, *haole* now means a Caucasian person.

hapa—a part, sometimes a half.

hapa haole—part *haole*, a person of mixed racial background, part of which is Caucasian.

hauoli—to rejoice. *Hauoli Makahiki Hou* means Happy New Year.

heiau—an ancient Hawaiian place of worship.

holo—to run.

holoholo—to go for a walk, ride, or sail.

holoku—a long Hawaiian dress, somewhat fitted, with a scoop neck and a train. Influenced by European fashion, it was worn at court.

holomuu—a recent cross between a *holoku* and a *muumuu*, less fitted than the former but less voluminous than the latter, and having no train.

honi—to kiss, a kiss. A phrase that some tourists may find useful, quoted from a popular *hula*, is *Honi Kaua wikiwiki:* Kiss me quick!

hoomalimali—flattery, a deceptive "line," bunk, baloney, hooey.

huhu—angry.

hui—a group, club, or assembly. There are church *huis* and social *huis*.

hukilau—a seine; a communal fishing party in which everyone helps to drive the fish into a huge net, pull it in, and divide the catch.

hula—the dance of Hawaii.

ipo—sweetheart.

ka—the definite article.

kahuna—a priest, doctor, or other trained person of old Hawaii, endowed with special professional skills that often included the gift of prophecy or other supernatural powers.

kai—the sea, salt water.

kalo—the taro plant from whose rokt *poi* is mada.

kamaaina—literally a child of the soil, it refers to people who were born in the Islands or have lived there for a long time.

kanaka—originally a man or humanity in general, it is now used to denote a male Hawaiian or part-Hawaiian.

kane—a man, a husband. If you see this word on a door, it's the men's room.

kapa—also called *tapa*, a cloth made of beaten bark and usually dyed and stamped with a geometric design.

kapakahi—crooked, cockeyed, uneven. You've got your hat on *kapakahi*.

kapu—keep out, prohibited. This is the Hawaiian version of the more widely known Tongan word *tabu* (taboo).

keiki—a child; *keikikane* is a boy child, *keikiwahine* a girl.

kona—the south, also the south or leeward side of the islands from which the *kona* wind and *kona* rain come.

kuleana—a homestead or small plot of ground on which a family has been installed for some generations without necessarily owning it. By extension, *kuleana* is used to denote any area or department in which one has a special interest or prerogative. You'll hear it used this way: If you want to hire a surfboard, see Moki; that's his *kuleana*. And conversely, I can't help you with that; that's not my *kuleana*.

lamalama—to fish with a torch.

lanai—a porch, a balcony, an outdoor living room. Almost every house in Hawaii has one.

lani—heaven, the sky.

lauhala—the leaf of the *hala* or pandanus tree, widely used in Hawaiian handcrafts.

lei—a garland of flowers.

luna—a plantation overseer or foreman.

mahalo—thank you.

makai—toward the ocean.

malihini—a newcomer to the Islands.

mana—the spiritual power that the Hawaiians believed to inhabit all things and creatures.

manawahi—free, gratis.

mauka—toward the mountains.

mauna—mountain.

mele—a Hawaiian song or chant, often of epic proportions.

menehune—a Hawaiian pixie. The *menehunes* were a legendary race of little people who accomplished prodigious work, such as building fish ponds and temples in the course of a single night.

moana—the ocean.

muumuu—the voluminous dress in which the missionaries enveloped Hawaiian women. Now made in bright printed cottons and silks, it is an indispensable garment in a Hawaiian woman's wardrobe.

nani—beautiful.

nui—big.

pake—Chinese. This *pake* craftsman makes beautiful things.

palapala—book, printing.

pali—a cliff, precipice.

panini—cactus.

paniolo—a Hawaiian cowboy.

pau—finished, done.

pilikia—trouble. The Hawaiian word is much more widely used here than its English equivalent.

puka—a hole.

pupule—crazy, like the celebrated Princess Pupule. This word has replaced its English equivalent in local usage.

wahine—a female, a woman, a wife, and a sign on the ladies' room door.

wai—fresh water, as opposed to salt water, which is *kai*.

wikiwiki—to hurry, hurry up.

Pidgin English is the unofficial language of Hawaii. It is heard everywhere: on ranches, in warehouses, on beaches, and in the hallowed halls (though not in the classrooms) of the University of Hawaii. It's still English and not much tougher to follow than Brooklynese; it just takes a little getting used to.

Menu Guide

Much of the Hawaiian language encountered during a stay in the Islands will appear on restaurant menus and lists of luau fare. Often these menus will also include terms from Japanese, Chinese, and other cultures. Here's a quick primer.

ahi—locally caught tuna.

aku—skipjack, bonito tuna.

ama ama—mullet; it's hard to get, but tasty.

bento—a box lunch.

dim sum—Chinese dumplings.

chicken luau—a stew made from chicken, taro leaves, and coconut milk.

guava—This tasty fruit is most often used in juice and in jellies. As a juice, it's pink and quenches a thirst like nothing else.

haupia—a light, gelatinlike dessert made from coconut.

imu—the underground ovens in which pigs are roasted for luaus.

kalua—to bake underground. A *kalua* pig is the pièce de résistance of a Hawaiian feast.

kaukau—food. The word's derivation is Chinese, but it is widely used in the Islands.

kim chee—pickled Chinese cabbage made with garlic and hot peppers.

kona coffee—coffee grown in the Kona district of the Big Island; prized for its rich flavor.

laulau—literally, a bundle. In everyday usage, laulaus are morsels of pork, butterfish, or other ingredients wrapped along with young taro shoots in ti leaves for steaming.

lilikoi (passion fruit)—a tart, seedy yellow fruit that makes delicious desserts, jellies, and sherbet.

lomilomi—to rub or massage; also a massage. Lomilomi salmon is fish that has been rubbed with onions and herbs, commonly served with minced onions and tomatoes.

luau—a Hawaiian feast, also the leaf of the taro plant used in preparing such a feast.

luau leaves—cooked taro tops with a taste similar to spinach.

macadamia nuts—These little round, buttery-tasting nuts are mostly grown on the Big Island, but are available throughout the Islands.

mahimahi—mild-flavored dolphin, not to be confused with porpoise.

mai tai—Hawaiian fruit punch with rum.

malasada—a Portuguese deep-fried doughnut, dipped in sugar, with no hole.

manapua—dough wrapped around diced pork.

mango—a juicy sweet fruit, with a yellowish-red smooth skin and a yellow pulpy interor.

mano—shark.

niu—coconut.

okolehao—a liqueur distilled from the ti root.

onaga—pink snapper.

ono (adj.)—delicious.

ono (n.)—a long, slender mackerel-like fish; also called a wahoo.

opakapaka—blue snapper.

opihi—a tiny shellfish, or mollusk, found on rocks; also called limpets.

papaya—This little green or yellow melon-like fruit will grow on you; it's high in vitamin C and is most often eaten at breakfast with a squeeze of lemon or lime.

papio—a young ulua or jack fish.

poha—Cape gooseberry. Tasting a bit like honey, the poha berry is often used in jams and desserts.

poi—a paste made from pounded taro root, a staple of the Hawaiian diet.

pupu—Hawaiian hors d'oeuvre.

saimin—long thin noodles and vegetables in a thin broth.

sashimi—raw fish sliced thin, usually eaten with soy sauce.

sushi—a variety of raw fish, served with vinegared rice and Japanese horseradish.

uku—deep-sea snapper.

ulua—crevelle, or jack fish; the giant trevally.

Index

Whale-watching, 63–64
The Wharf (shopping center), 68
Windjammer Cruises, 113

Windmill Beach, *81*
Windsurfing, *58, 75, 82*
Windsurfing, professional, *83*
Wineries, *56, 71*

Wo Hing Society, *49*
Woolworth (shop), *71*
World Gym, *78*
Wyland Galleries, *69*

Yee's Orchard, *64*

YMCA, *110*
Youth hostels, *110*

Zoos, *51–52*

Personal Itinerary

Departure *Date*

Time

Transportation

Arrival *Date*   *Time*

Departure *Date*   *Time*

Transportation

Accommodations

Arrival *Date*   *Time*

Departure *Date*   *Time*

Transportation

Accommodations

Arrival *Date*   *Time*

Departure *Date*   *Time*

Transportation

Accommodations

Personal Itinerary

Arrival	*Date*	*Time*
Departure	*Date*	*Time*
Transportation		
Accommodations		

Arrival	*Date*	*Time*
Departure	*Date*	*Time*
Transportation		
Accommodations		

Arrival	*Date*	*Time*
Departure	*Date*	*Time*
Transportation		
Accommodations		

Arrival	*Date*	*Time*
Departure	*Date*	*Time*
Transportation		
Accommodations		

Personal Itinerary

Arrival *Date*   *Time*

Departure *Date*   *Time*

Transportation

Accommodations

Arrival *Date*   *Time*

Departure *Date*   *Time*

Transportation

Accommodations

Arrival *Date*   *Time*

Departure *Date*   *Time*

Transportation

Accommodations

Arrival *Date*   *Time*

Departure *Date*   *Time*

Transportation

Accommodations

Personal Itinerary

Arrival *Date*   *Time*

Departure *Date*   *Time*

Transportation

Accommodations

Arrival *Date*   *Time*

Departure *Date*   *Time*

Transportation

Accommodations

Arrival *Date*   *Time*

Departure *Date*   *Time*

Transportation

Accommodations

Arrival *Date*   *Time*

Departure *Date*   *Time*

Transportation

Accommodations

Addresses

Name

Address

Telephone

Name

Address

Telephone

Name

Address

Telephone

Name

Address

Telephone

Name

Address

Telephone

Name

Address

Telephone

Name

Address

Telephone

Name

Address

Telephone

Name

Address

Telephone

Name

Address

Telephone

Name

Address

Telephone

Name

Address

Telephone

Name

Address

Telephone

Name

Address

Telephone

Name

Address

Telephone

Name

Address

Telephone

Addresses

Name	*Name*
Address	*Address*
Telephone	*Telephone*
Name	*Name*
Address	*Address*
Telephone	*Telephone*
Name	*Name*
Address	*Address*
Telephone	*Telephone*
Name	*Name*
Address	*Address*
Telephone	*Telephone*
Name	*Name*
Address	*Address*
Telephone	*Telephone*
Name	*Name*
Address	*Address*
Telephone	*Telephone*
Name	*Name*
Address	*Address*
Telephone	*Telephone*
Name	*Name*
Address	*Address*
Telephone	*Telephone*

Notes

Fodor's Travel Guides

U.S. Guides

Alaska
Arizona
Boston
California
Cape Cod
The Carolinas & the
  Georgia Coast
The Chesapeake
  Region
Chicago
Colorado
Disney World & the
  Orlando Area
Florida
Hawaii
Las Vegas, Reno,
  Tahoe

Los Angeles
Maine, New
  Hampshire &
  Vermont
Maui
Miami & the
  Keys
National Parks
  of the West
New England
New Mexico
New Orleans
New York City
New York City
  (Pocket Guide)
Norway
Pacific North Coast

Philadelphia & the
  Pennsylvania
  Dutch Country
Puerto Rico
  (Pocket Guide)
The Rockies
San Diego
San Francisco
San Francisco
  (Pocket Guide)
The South
Santa, Fe Taos,
  Albuquerque
Seattle &
  Vancouver
Texas
USA

The U. S. & British
  Virgin Islands
The Upper Great
  Lakes Region
Vacations in
  New York State
Vacations on the
  Jersey Shore
Virginia & Maryland
Waikiki
Washington, D.C.

Foreign Guides

Acapulco
Amsterdam
Australia
Austria
The Bahamas
The Bahamas
  (Pocket Guide)
Baja & Mexico's Pacific
  Coast Resorts
Barbados
Barcelona, Madrid,
  Seville
Belgium &
  Luxembourg
Berlin
Bermuda
Brazil
Budapest
Budget Europe
Canada
Canada's Atlantic
  Provinces

Cancun, Cozumel,
  Yucatan Peninsula
Caribbean
Central America
China
Eastern Europe
Egypt
Europe
Europe's Great Cities
France
Germany
Great Britain
Greece
The Himalayan
  Countries
Holland
Hong Kong
India
Ireland
Israel
Italy
Italy 's Great Cities

Jamaica
Japan
Kenya, Tanzania,
  Seychelles
Korea
London
London
  (Pocket Guide)
London Companion
Mexico
Mexico City
Montreal &
  Quebec City
Morocco
New Zealand
Nova Scotia,
  New Brunswick,
  Prince Edward
  Island
Paris
Paris (Pocket Guide)
Portugal

Prague
Rio
Rome
Scandinavia
Scandinavian Cities
Scotland
Singapore
South America
South Pacific
Southeast Asia
Soviet Union
Spain
Sweden
Switzerland
Sydney
Thailand
Tokyo
Toronto
Turkey
Vienna
Yugoslavia

Wall Street Journal Guides to Business Travel

Europe | International Cities | Pacific Rim | USA & Canada

Special-Interest Guides

Bed & Breakfasts and
  Country Inns:
  Mid-Atlantic Region
Bed & Breakfasts and
  Country Inns:
  New England

Cruises and Ports
  of Call
Healthy Escapes
Fodor's Flashmaps
  New York

Fodor's Flashmaps
  Washington, D.C.
Shopping in Europe
Skiing in the U.S. &
  Canada

Smart Shopper's
  Guide to London
Sunday in New York
Touring Europe